THE
NEW YORKER

ENCYCLOPEDIA OF CARTOONS
VOLUME I

THE
NEW YORKER

ENCYCLOPEDIA OF CARTOONS
VOLUME I

FOREWORD BY DAVID REMNICK
EDITED BY BOB MANKOFF

Black Dog & Leventhal Publishers
Hachette Book Group
1290 Avenue of the Americas
New York, NY 10104
www.hachettebookgroup.com
www.blackdogandleventhal.com

First Edition: October 2018
Black Dog & Leventhal Publishers is an imprint of Hachette Books,
a division of Hachette Book Group. The Black Dog & Leventhal Publishers
name and logo are trademarks of Hachette Book Group, Inc.

The publisher is not responsible for websites (or their content)
that are not owned by the publisher.

The Hachette Speakers Bureau provides a wide range of authors for speaking events.
To find out more, go to www.HachetteSpeakersBureau.com or call (866) 376-6591.

Book interior design by Eight and a Half, NY, Ltd. 8point5.com

To purchase prints of cartoons, please visit The New Yorker Store,
at https://condenaststore.com/conde-nast-brand/thenewyorker
To license cartoons, visit The Cartoon Bank, a division of Condé Nast,
at www.cartoonbank.com, or contact The Cartoon Bank at
1 World Trade Center, 29th Fl., New York, NY 10007;
phone: 1-800-897-8666; e-mail: image_licensing@condenast.com

The Cartoon Bank® is a registered trademark of Condé Nast,
a division of Advance Magazine Publishers Inc.

Library of Congress Control Number: 2017956541
ISBNs: 978-0-316-43667-0 (hardcover); 978-0-316-43666-3 (deluxe edition); 978-0-316-43665-6 (ebook)
Printed in China
IM
10 9 8 7 6 5 4 3 2 1

"I tell you, the book has everything—
sex, history, consciousness, and cats!"

WILLIAM HAMILTON, APRIL 11, 1977

FOREWORD

BY DAVID REMNICK

I F MY APARTMENT were ablaze and my family safely on the street, the only reason I might charge back through the door would be to rescue a fortieth-birthday present that my colleagues at *The New Yorker* gave me shortly before I went home one late October night to contemplate the onset of middle age and my own senescence.

The gift hangs (framed and a little cockeyed) in our hallway; it's an original cartoon strip called "Charles Addams," written and drawn by the modern master Roz Chast. Eleven panels long, the strip is one of the best descriptions I've encountered of how artistic influence happens. Roz tells of how her parents, a pair of eccentric Brooklyn schoolteachers, would take her along to Cornell University, in upstate New York, for the summer and, while they indulged in "a certain degree of intellectualism"—lectures, courses, and the like—Roz stashed herself away in a corner of Cornell's lending library. No reason to feel sorry for her. Roz is not what you would call an outdoorsy type. I am quite sure that her favorite form of flora is the fire hydrant. She was quite content not to be forced into getting any fresh air. City kids of her stripe prefer stale air, air-conditioned air—anything but fresh air. The library was a paper paradise. Roz immersed herself in the collection's many cartoon books, the works of such *New Yorker* artists as Helen Hokinson, Otto Soglow, and George Price.

"But the books I was obsessed with were by Charles Addams," she writes in the strip. "'Monster Rally,' 'Black Maria,' 'Homebodies,' 'Nightcrawlers,' 'Drawn and Quartered'. . . I laughed at everything that I knew I shouldn't find funny: homicidal spouses, kids building guillotines in their rooms, and all those poor, unfortunate two-headed, three-legged, four-armed people."

Addams, with his spooky characters and "sick jokes," introduced Roz to grown-up humor and the joys of impropriety. This was before the rise of the parental admonition "That is so *inappropriate*." Roz loved inappropriate, and she found it, boundlessly, in Addams. One of her favorite Addams cartoons was

the captionless drawing known as "Boiling Oil," in which Morticia, Gomez, and Lurch, members of the artist's signature family of creepy goths, perch on the roof of their house and, with murderous, seasonal glee, tip an overflowing cauldron onto the merry carolers below. Perfect for the holidays! Or so one might have thought. In the winter of 1946, Addams, working with Peter De Vries, proposed this idea as a Christmas cover to the magazine's founding editor, Harold Ross, but Ross, fearing a reader rebellion, said no. He played it safe and used it inside the magazine. Big mistake.

To the lonely, goggle-eyed scholar of *New Yorker* cartoons—and there are surely doctoral dissertations being ground out at this very moment—the Chast strip on Addams is gold; it's a Rosetta stone, a Dead Sea scroll. Influence, admittedly, is a weird and imprecise business. Roz also used to curl up as a child with another thick book, the Merck manual, and, I think, Jules Feiffer and Mary Petty also fit into the Venn diagram of what helped make Chast the great artist of urban mishegoss. Addams came by his ghoulish predilections, at least in part, while working at *True Detective* in the nineteen-thirties. As a member of the layout staff, he was charged with retouching photographs of corpses, removing any overly garish blood. "A lot of those corpses were more interesting the way they were," he maintained.

Right from the start, these cartoons make you wonder: Why are there so many desert islands and talking dogs in *New Yorker* cartoons? Why are horses so weary and cats so wise? I started trying to figure out this stuff many years ago—long before it became my routine to meet with the cartoon editor on Wednesday afternoons to select fifteen or twenty drawings from a stack of up to a hundred. My father had a small dental practice in our house, and on mornings when he wasn't working I went down to the waiting room, where, sitting on the cool linoleum floor, I read stacks of magazines intended to distract his patients from their painful anticipatory fantasies. I was nine or ten and, believe me, I wasn't reading

The New Yorker for its coverage of Vietnam or the civil-rights movement. But I did like those strange cartoons. They seemed to me a great deal funnier than the strips that ran in our local paper. And more distinctive, mysterious, mischievous. After a while, I began to sense that each artist had his or her own look; they each had a vocabulary, recurring images, a particularized world. There were realists, surrealists, one-liner gagsters, wordless absurdists, kitchen-table moralists. Some provided lessons; others wouldn't be caught dead doing so. Some were of the moment; others operated utterly outside of time. William Steig hardly seemed a cartoonist at all; Saul Steinberg appeared to be a gnomic genius who existed beyond the genre and the magazine itself. And yet I found even my frequent incomprehension enjoyable. Sprawled out alone in my father's waiting room, I was learning a language, and always laughing. Sometimes the cartoonists were speaking less to the reader than to other cartoonists. Some were in dialogue with their influences, as Roz Chast was with Charles Addams.

Figuring out who comes from whom and what comes from what, trying to learn that limitless language of cartoons, its many dialects, is, I hope, part of the fun of this colossal encyclopedia. Cartooning has a long pre–*New Yorker* history. James Gillray, William Hogarth, George Cruikshank, Honoré Daumier, Thomas Nast, Leslie Ward, Carlo Pellegrini, Max Beerbohm: they were all cartoonists of a kind. But with the launch of the magazine, in 1925, cartooning in America, particularly of the one-panel, one-gag variety, began to center increasingly on one source, one publication. The magazine did not always shoulder such a singular role. In the early days, *The New Yorker* faced stiff competition; artists had many places to go with their work. But, as magazines closed, *The New Yorker* became the home for many: Helen Hokinson, Gardner Rea, James Thurber, Alan Dunn, George Price, Peter Arno, Chon Day, William Steig, Whitney Darrow Jr., Saul Steinberg, Frank Modell—and, of course, the luminously antic talents of later generations.

Any cartoon compilation that draws from these archives makes it clear what a male preserve it was. As late as 1981, the magazine had contracts with forty cartoonists—thirty-nine men and one woman. (Liza Donnelly's book *Funny Ladies* is particularly sharp both in its critique and in its appreciation of the work of the women who did get through the doors.) Bob Mankoff, who was the cartoon editor from 1997 to 2017, promoted young stars like Emily Flake, Julia Suits, and Liana Finck, and his successor, Emma Allen, has accelerated the effort to draw from a more diverse assemblage of talent. Cartoonists poke fun at the absurdities of their day, but, as a guild, they're not necessarily free of them.

A caution to the reader: The usual way to come across *New Yorker* cartoons is in the magazine or, more recently, on newyorker.com and on social media. There's something distinctive, maybe even perverse, about the experience of glancing away from a long piece about, say, a particularly dusty province of the Middle East to drink quickly from the oasis of a good cartoon. To get a gazillion of them all at once, as you do here, runs a certain risk of overindulgence. So, please: Read in spurts. Visit far-flung themes. Skip around. Screw around. Read randomly, irresponsibly. But not straight through. Lee Lorenz, who was Bob Mankoff's predecessor as cartoon editor, once calculated that he used to review up to three thousand ideas a week and that, over the years, he had looked at two and a half million. Just as the seventh cheeseburger may be somewhat less delicious than the first, it is entirely possible that the optimal way to confront this two-volume compendium of joy is not to soldier through from start to finish. This could tip into earnest obligation. And you've got enough in your life that's obligatory. I don't even know you, and I know that much.

Instead, think of yourself as the young Roz Chast, curled up in an armchair somewhere in Ithaca, reading purely for pleasure, flipping and zipping around, with no adults around to rush you or recommend anything. Be a kid again; go back in time. This book could save your life… or, at least, prolong it.

INTRODUCTION

BY BOB MANKOFF

CARTOONS HAVE A history, and sometimes that history is the cartoon's real topic. Whatever else they're about, each new Adam and Eve, Crash Test Dummy, or Desert Island cartoon is also about all those that preceded it. Encyclopedias, too, have a history, typically accessible in, whaddyaknow, Volume E. Now, as it happens, I have a history with both cartooning and encyclopedias. I guess that's how I wound up assembling a cartoon encyclopedia.

Having been *The New Yorker*'s cartoon editor for two decades and published cartoons in *The New Yorker* for four decades, I can readily establish my bona fides on the first point. But there's more: Back in the nineteen-seventies, I did a stint selling encyclopedias door to door. It was bruising, both for the back and for the ego. I'd knock on the door with my samples, and usually what I'd hear was: *Not interested.* This turned out to be excellent practice for peddling cartoons to *The New Yorker*, because that's pretty much all I heard for the first three years that I submitted my work there.

In the end, I had more luck selling cartoons than encyclopedias, but my fascination with the latter was the real deal. It still is. Maybe that's because, never having learned what I was supposed to have learned when I was supposed to have learned it, I've spent the rest of my life compensating. And what better place for a compulsive autodidact than an encyclopedia, with its one easily digestible morsel of knowledge after another after another. (Bet you can't learn just one.)

The form is irresistible, too: there's the beautiful arbitrariness of alphabetical organization, which allows for utterly incongruous juxtapositions. Then there's the very substantiality of these works, their physical heft. Really, you could do reps with one of those old-time tomes—try that with Wikipedia.

If encyclopedias are heavy, cartoons are light, and yet they, too, can pull some weight. *New Yorker* cartoons evolve along with everything else in our culture, but here we're going to revisit the glories of those classic tropes, tableaux, and themes that people have enjoyed for generations. Think of this as the Great American Songbook of cartoons. Or as a way of listening in to a decades-long conversation among cartoonists. Comic conceits drift and shift. They get polished and simplified over time, or roughed up and complicated. They get mashed up, mixed up, updated, and reversed. They lose their innocence; they become self-reflexive.

Images become icons, and icons get smashed. A famous picture like Charles Addams's pair of ski tracks swerving around a tree could become riff fodder for later cartoons; still later cartoons could riff on the riff. "I say it's spinach, and I say the hell with it" could become "I say it's genetically modified broccoli, and I say the hell with it." Mischief and inventiveness yield playful homage. In a celebrated essay, George Orwell attacked cliché as the enemy of thought; how thoughtless of him. The cartoonist thinks by embracing clichés, recklessly playing with them, upgrading them to tropes, and not worrying about it all becoming *de trop*. And, believe me, Mr. Orwell, when the results come together they're worth every other penny.

The zone between familiarity and novelty, then, is the microclimate where cartoonists flourish. Some themes you can carbon-date with precision. Grim Reapers start haunting our cartoons in 1967, Crash Test Dummies first slammed into our panels in 1993, and the first Beached Whale cartoon came to our shores in 1998. More themes follow, in the spirit of "Game on." You'll see (and read) more about this process in the pages of this collection.

If cartoonists are always playing with the form of the cartoon, a cartoon encyclopedia is bound to play with the form of the encyclopedia. This isn't play for its own sake, of course. A cartoon, unlike serious art, has a specific burden: it has to be funny. A cartoon encyclopedia is, in turn, a cartoon of an encyclopedia; it requires that you ignore most of reality, entertain a belief in impossible things, and enter another world—a world that's as real and as fake as this encyclopedia. Where, you lament, are the jokes about nineteen-seventies stagflation? And how, you nitpick, could we have included Elvis and left out elves?

HOW WE DO IT (A WEEK IN THE LIFE OF A NEW YORKER CARTOONIST) BY JOE DATOR

EVERY NEW YORKER CARTOONIST IS REQUIRED TO CREATE ONE (1) HILARIOUS NEW CARTOON PER WEEK. THIS PROCESS BEGINS EARLY WEDNESDAY MORNING.

AFTER BREAKFAST WE SLIDE DOWN THE CARTOONIST POLES FROM OUR GRAND SUITES HIGH ATOP THE NEW YORKER BUILDING AND GET TO WORK.

EACH OF US HAS A FULLY EQUIPPED OFFICE, WITH A STAFF OF RESEARCH ASSISTANTS WHO HELP US GATHER MATERIAL FOR IDEAS.

BY THURSDAY IT'S TIME TO TURN THAT MATERIAL INTO ONE (1) HILARIOUS CARTOON. THIS IS WHAT WE CALL "THE EASY PART", AND THURSDAY IS ALMOST ALWAYS A HALF DAY.

FRIDAY IS A DAY OFF, WE SPEND THE REST OF THE WEEKEND UNWINDING WITH MERRY SPORT. MONDAY IS ALSO A DAY OFF.

ON TUESDAY WE SHOW OUR WORK TO THE CARTOON EDITOR, WHEN HE FINISHES LAUGHING (10-30 MINUTES, USUALLY) HE HANDS US AN ATTACHÉ CASE FULL OF MONEY OR PRECIOUS GEMS.

ON RARE OCCASIONS A CARTOON MAY NOT BE ACCEPTED FOR PUBLICATION. WHEN THIS HAPPENS THERE IS A SUPPORT TEAM READY TO HELP US PROCESS THE LOSS.

FINALLY THE CARTOON IS PUBLISHED. AFTER A SERIES OF CELEBRATORY EVENTS, AND A BRIEF VACATION, OUR WEEKLY GRIND BEGINS AGAIN!

JOE DATOR, SEPTEMBER 4, 2012

See under "A" for arbitrary, "B" for bushwa, and "C" for caprice. A cartoon asks only that you go along with its premise; so does a cartoon encyclopedia.

When you're stooped over a blank page or screen, cartooning can seem a lonely enterprise. But the fact is that you're not alone; you're part of a collective creative enterprise, bounded by long-standing traditions and buoyed by the always-changing zeitgeist. The genius of cartooning is really collective: you commune with everyone else who has worked in the form. All of which is to say that those at work today are standing on the shoulders of others, who are standing on—hey, it's shoulders all the way down to whoever beautifully defaced those caves at Lascaux.

The same principle of collaboration goes for encyclopedias. I couldn't have assembled this one without the help of David Remnick, Pam McCarthy, Henry Finder, Nicholas Blechman, Eric Simonoff, Colin Stokes, Trevor Hoey, Sharan Shetty, Mary Hawthorne, Kate Norris, Eleanor Martin, Jessie Hunnicutt, J. P. Leventhal, Becky Koh, and Bonnie Siegler—and, behind all of us, the generations of editors and cartoonists and readers who created the ethos of *The New Yorker* and made all this material possible. Special thanks to those talented souls who joined me to craft the brief commentaries you'll encounter: Pat Byrnes, Emily Flake, Paul Karasik, Tom Toro, and Colin Stokes.

ED FISHER, MAY 30, 1959

ACCOUNTANTS
ADAM & EVE
ADULTERY
ADVERTISING
AGING
AIR TRAVEL
ALTERNATIVE ENERGY
AMERICAN HISTORY
ARCHAEOLOGY
ARCHITECTURE
ARTISTS
ASTRONOMY
ATLAS
AUTOMATION

"We are neither hunters nor gatherers. We are accountants."

"Accountant."

TOP SAM GROSS, JANUARY 11, 1993 BOTTOM CHRISTOPHER WEYANT, AUGUST 19, 2002

"And to think he started in accounting."

ROBERT WEBER, DECEMBER 4, 2000

"First rule—what happens in accounting stays in accounting."

"The whole fun of accounting was that willingness to suspend disbelief."

TOP TOM CHENEY, MAY 12, 2008   BOTTOM WILLIAM HAMILTON, SEPTEMBER 1, 2003

"Run it by legal."   "Run it by accounting."

TOP ROZ CHAST, JUNE 28, 2010   BOTTOM ALEX GREGORY, OCTOBER 15, 2007

"I can't help thinking there's a book in this."

"No one said we couldn't eat the snake."

TOP MICK STEVENS, AUGUST 2, 1999   BOTTOM MICHAEL SHAW, AUGUST 9, 2010

"Hey, Adam! A talking snake!"

ED FISHER, MARCH 14, 1964

"Frankly, I think we'll regret introducing these organisms into the environment."

"At least we don't have to sit through some big, prolonged trial."

TOP LEE LORENZ, JULY 27, 1987   BOTTOM JACK ZIEGLER, NOVEMBER 22, 1999

"Just for the record, I knew you were naked <u>before</u> I ate the apple."

TOP BILL WOODMAN, JULY 22, 1996   BOTTOM LEE LORENZ, AUGUST 6, 2001

"So you think I should just ignore it?"

*"What I don't, like, get is how she, like, figured out I was,
like, having an affair with, like, the babysitter."*

TOP BRUCE KAPLAN, FEBRUARY 20, 1995   BOTTOM DANNY SHANAHAN, JANUARY 8, 2001

"Well, what you call an affair I prefer to call an anomaly."

"Oh, all right, dear. For the sake of argument,
let's say there is another woman, whom I'll call Muffy."

TOP BOB MANKOFF, MAY 19, 1997   BOTTOM WILLIAM HAMILTON, JULY 21, 1997

"Not on the mattress where we keep all our money!"

"Helen, I really wish you would respect my creative process."

TOP FRANK COTHAM, OCTOBER 6, 2008   BOTTOM CHRISTOPHER WEYANT, MAY 7, 2007

*SEE ALSO DIVORCE, ETHICS, LAWYERS

"I can explain everything."

"I think that just my being here is a big mistake."

TOP SAM GROSS, OCTOBER 1, 2001   BOTTOM DANNY SHANAHAN, APRIL 21, 1997

"How else are we going to pay for the war?"

"I used to be in advertising. Remember 'Buy this, you morons'?
That was mine."

TOP ALEX GREGORY, OCTOBER, 7 2002 BOTTOM ROBERT WEBER, OCTOBER 4, 1993

"I'm in advertising."

"I like it. It's dumb without trying to be clever."

"Let me see the first one again."

TOP MATTHEW DIFFEE, OCTOBER 22, 2007   MIDDLE WARREN MILLER, FEBRUARY 8, 1993   BOTTOM TOM CHENEY, DECEMBER 21, 1992

BETTER THAN EVER

THE STORY GOES that the Ad Man made a pact with the devil, through which he gained the devil's ability to misrepresent. He instantly applied this skill. The devil walked away believing that there was actually a difference between Charmin and Cottonelle toilet paper. The poor devil did not get the Ad Man's soul. **The Ad Man has no soul.**

Like toilet paper, Ad Men come in several varieties, but all are aimed at the same end. Their differences make them highly riffable as fodder for gags. One running theme is cluelessness; often, our marketers are guileless dopes who resemble nothing so much as an alarmed group of chickens, albeit festooned with pince-nez and pocket watches. Another species is the slimeball, who so loathes his fellow man that he slaps "New" and "Improved" labels on the same crap he's been peddling for years. But those are the easy targets. The Ad Man cartoon doesn't shy away from skewering the gullible, corrupted consumer, eager to be sold short at every turn. ◆

EDWARD KOREN, NOVEMBER 17, 1986

"You don't get it, Daddy, because they're not targeting you."

TOP WILLIAM HAMILTON, APRIL 10, 1995   BOTTOM PAUL NOTH, JULY 7, 2008

"Actually, I preferred 'Heaven,' too, but then the marketing guys got hold of it."

"Unfortunately, a few years back we had to start accepting advertising."

TOP LEE LORENZ, DECEMBER 15, 1997   BOTTOM MICK STEVENS, NOVEMBER 25, 2002

*"No, I don't want to live forever,
but I damn sure don't want to be dead forever, either."*

"If I were a dog I'd only be nine years old."

TOP BOB MANKOFF, DECEMBER 8, 1997   BOTTOM ROBERT WEBER, NOVEMBER 13, 1989

"*Good news, honey—seventy is the new fifty.*"

TOP ROZ CHAST, JANUARY 19, 1998   BOTTOM VICTORIA ROBERTS, JUNE 5, 2000

MARISA ACOCELLA, AUGUST 7, 2000

SIPRESS

"I come from the future."

"Then one day I woke up and just couldn't do perky anymore."

TOP DAVID SIPRESS, DECEMBER 20, 1999 BOTTOM DONALD REILLY, FEBRUARY 7, 1994

"I'm turning into my mother."

"One senior and one refuses to accept he's a senior."

TOP PAUL NOTH, AUGUST 28, 2006 BOTTOM DAVID SIPRESS, AUGUST 4, 2008

"Today I'm fifty—the old halfway point."

FROM ZERO TO SIXTY
IN WHAT SEEMS LIKE EIGHT SECONDS FLAT

TOP ROBERT WEBER, SEPTEMBER 5, 1988   BOTTOM PETER STEINER, MAY 3, 1993

"Why didn't you bring a cardigan or lightweight jacket?"

TOP ROZ CHAST, DECEMBER 16, 1991   BOTTOM JOE DATOR, OCTOBER 8, 2007

"It's been nice talking to you, but I should probably get
back to staring blankly ahead."

TOP ALEX GREGORY, MARCH 13, 2006   BOTTOM MORT GERBER, JULY 4, 1970

"Attention passengers. Flight 369 has been cancelled due to our desire to ruin your life."

TOP CHRISTOPHER WEYANT, DECEMBER 20, 2010   MIDDLE JACK ZIEGLER, NOVEMBER 21, 1994   BOTTOM MATTHEW DIFFEE, AUGUST 16, 1999

"I always get stuck in the wrong line."

"Yeah, but it doesn't smell like a bomb!"

TOP DREW DERNAVICH, NOVEMBER 18, 2013   BOTTOM FRANK COTHAM, FEBRUARY 24, 1997

"It saves energy and makes me feel holier."

Solar-Powered Catnap

TOP LEO CULLUM, SEPTEMBER 8, 2008   BOTTOM JASON PATTERSON, AUGUST 24, 2009

"I miss the palm tree, also, but at least we can have a refrigerator."

SAM GROSS, JUNE 8, 2009

"I cook everything with an alternative energy source, so it may take a while."

ANOTHER ENERGY-SAVING IDEA FROM YOUR ELECTRIC-EEL COUNCIL

TOP P.C. VEY, AUGUST 25, 2008   BOTTOM BOB MANKOFF, DECEMBER 3, 1990

"Don't we have lighting more intimidating than that energy saver?"

TOP NICULAE ASCIU, MARCH 29, 1976   BOTTOM DREW DERNAVICH, JUNE 1, 2009

"We'll be paying for the prairie, the forests, and the streams with this credit card, which is just as good as—if not better than—trinkets."

"Actually, the attraction wasn't freedom from religious persecution but, rather, the all-you-can-eat buffet."

TOP JACK ZIEGLER, MAY 29, 2006   BOTTOM CHRISTOPHER WEYANT, NOVEMBER 29, 1999

*"I wonder if future generations will realize that
their forefathers were such gun nuts?"*

"Founding Fathers! How come no Founding Mothers?"

TOP CHRISTOPHER WEYANT, JULY 1, 2002   BOTTOM DANA FRADON, JULY 29, 1972

"*You know, the idea of taxation with representation doesn't appeal to me very much, either.*"

"*Thanks, but what about those silver candlesticks I ordered?*"

"*Religious freedom is my immediate goal, but my long-range plan is to go into real estate.*"

TOP J.B. HANDELSMAN, JUNE 27, 1970   MIDDLE PETER ARNO, JUNE 8, 1957   BOTTOM DONALD REILLY, JUNE 3, 1974

"O.K., the third of July is out. How about the fourth?"

PETER STEINER, JULY 8, 1996

COACHING THE LITTLE GIANT

"O.K. Now, if he comes at you with 'A house divided against itself cannot stand,' what's your reply?"

"Don't worry. If it turns out tobacco is harmful, we can always quit."

TOP ED FISHER, OCTOBER 26, 1992   BOTTOM GARRETT PRICE, FEBRUARY 22, 1958

"I thought I was going to be much more blown away by the Liberty Bell."

*"'Give me liberty or give me death.'
Now, what kind of person would say something like that?"*

TOP BRUCE KAPLAN, AUGUST 6, 2007   BOTTOM ROBERT WEBER, SEPTEMBER 6, 1993

*"Don't worry—we're merely employees.
The curse would apply to the Foundation."*

TOP CHON DAY, SEPTEMBER 8, 1956   BOTTOM CHARLES ADDAMS, OCTOBER 8, 1960

*"Think it over. One statue sold to one museum,
or a dozen fragments sold to a dozen museums."*

*"It doesn't mean a thing, but boy, will it drive
them crazy a thousand years from now!"*

TOP ALAN DUNN, MARCH 7, 1959   BOTTOM ED FISHER, JANUARY 26, 1963

"It's a real shame that once Tut's buried nobody will ever see this stuff again."

"Are you absolutely sure about this?"

TOP JAMES STEVENSON, OCTOBER 30, 1978   BOTTOM TOM CHENEY, DECEMBER 4, 1989

"I'm just plain stuck for a rhyme."

"If I read it right, it says, 'Wrapped by Operator No. 25.'"

TOP CARL ROSE, JANUARY 5, 1952   BOTTOM MISCHA RICHTER, NOVEMBER 15, 1960

"I guess cats just can't appreciate Frank Gehry."

TOP JAMES STEVENSON, AUGUST 16, 1976   BOTTOM ERIC LEWIS, SEPTEMBER 18, 2000

"*Great design, but, when the time comes, a bitch to implode.*"

"*What I'm trying to achieve for you is an eclectic mix of
classic B.C. and a touch or two of A.D. glitz.*"

TOP WARREN MILLER, MARCH 19, 2001   BOTTOM DONALD REILLY, APRIL 18, 1988

*"Once, I tried to change the laces, and the Landmarks Commission
came down on me like a ton of bricks."*

ALEX GREGORY, JUNE 12, 2000

*SEE ALSO EASTER ISLAND, HONEY I'M HOME, PYRAMIDS

"And, yet another plus, it will block out the sun's harmful ultraviolet rays from a considerable portion of the city."

TOP PETER PORGES, SEPTEMBER 2, 1967   BOTTOM DANA FRADON, NOVEMBER 2, 1992

"Workaholic? Brokers and salesmen are workaholics.
Artists are obsessed. There's a difference."

TOP WILLIAM STEIG, DECEMBER 26, 1988   BOTTOM EDWARD SOREL, APRIL 24, 1995

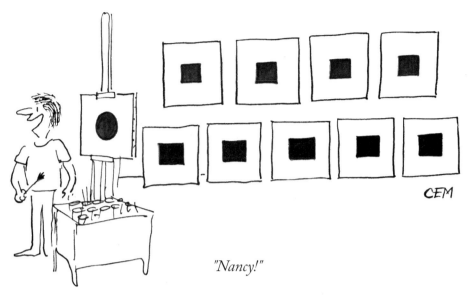

"Nancy!"

"I've lost track of the story."

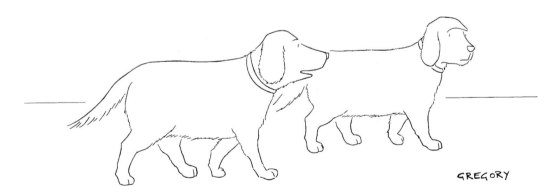

"What I do as an artist is take an ordinary object—say, a lamppost—and, by urinating on it, transform it into something that is uniquely my own."

TOP CHARLES MARTIN, MARCH 23, 1968   MIDDLE JAMES STEVENSON, MAY 25, 1981   BOTTOM ALEX GREGORY, APRIL 1, 2002

*"This artist is a deeply religious feminist and anti-smoking advocate,
who made a lot of money in the computer industry before going off to paint in Paris,
where she now lives with her husband and two little girls."*

"Of course you don't understand it. He's an artists' artist."

TOP DAVID SIPRESS, MAY 22, 2000   BOTTOM BARNEY TOBEY, FEBRUARY 12, 1979

*SEE ALSO BEATNIKS, CENSORSHIP, UNEMPLOYMENT

"They're no more pointless now than they ever were."

"It's meaningless, lady, believe me—I painted it."

TOP MIKE TWOHY, NOVEMBER 26, 2001   BOTTOM MICHAEL CRAWFORD, DECEMBER 3, 2007

"Yes, I'm sure. It says here the full moon isn't until the twenty-third."

*"Yes, a hole in space three hundred million light-years across does
make me pause and feel tiny and insignificant,
but a glance around at my peers usually restores my equanimity."*

TOP MICK STEVENS, NOVEMBER 5, 2001   BOTTOM DONALD REILLY, OCTOBER 24, 1988

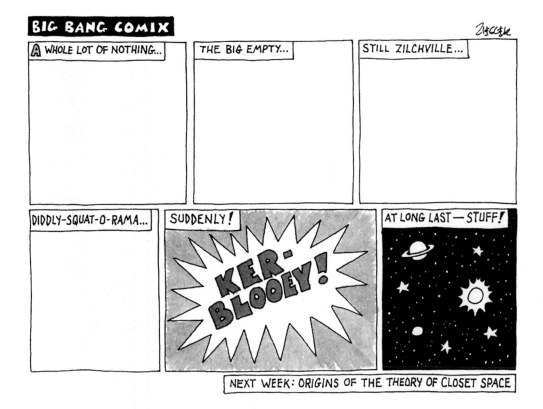

"See anything?"

TOP JACK ZIEGLER, JULY 6, 1992   BOTTOM ROBERT WEBER, APRIL 29, 1991

"Not good!"

"I want to see Halley's Comet, all right.
But I could skip the hype."

"Gosh, thanks, honey! If I discover a new star,
I'll name it after you."

TOP GAHAN WILSON, APRIL 28, 1980 MIDDLE ED FISHER, SEPTEMBER 9, 1985 BOTTOM BARNEY TOBEY, JUNE 20, 1977

"*Something goes around something, but that's as far as I've got.*"

JAMES STEVENSON, NOVEMBER 25, 1985

TOP LEO CULLUM, FEBRUARY 9, 2009   BOTTOM MISCHA RICHTER, JUNE 6, 1988

"It was believed back in those days that the world was flat."

TOP AL ROSS, JUNE 22, 1992   BOTTOM MISCHA RICHTER, JULY 6, 1963

"I can't believe I didn't think of this before."

TOP OTTO SOGLOW, JUNE 2, 1956   BOTTOM FARLEY KATZ, APRIL 5, 2010

BOB MANKOFF, APRIL 29, 1991

*"Before I forget, you had a call from a talking computer named Ted,
who is conducting an important homeowners' survey."*

TOP ROBERT DAY, JUNE 27, 1964   BOTTOM FRANK MODELL, APRIL 8, 1985

"I see Fenton's is finally automating."

TOP CHARLES ADDAMS, SEPTEMBER 28, 1981   BOTTOM DANA FRADON, MARCH 21, 1964

THE GHOST IN THE MACHINE

MAN VERSUS MACHINE. It's a conflict dating back to Daedalus, that mythical inventor of wings, labyrinths, and irony. **His creations solved problems but created even worse ones.** This cycle has frustrated humanity and fascinated cartoonists ever since. "By George, automation does create new jobs!" exclaims the boss in Alan Dunn's 1956 drawing of factory workers fixing a contraption that has replaced their colleagues. Automation economizes—but at what cost? Cartoonists, as manual laborers in the most literal sense, generally have a blue-collar bias. Ordinary folks—baffled, mistreated, suddenly obsolete—are protagonists pitted against the latest whizbang gizmos. Yes, resistance is futile. But futility is funny. Luddites are perfect comedic foils because underdogs are as American as apple pie—even if it's pie served from a Helen Hokinson coin-operated vending machine. Yet the question nags: do cartoonists really care? Jokes, after all, cannot be automated. There's no assembly line for one-liners. Humor just might be the final advantage humans have over machines—at least until robots realize they're the butt of our jokes and give us all the boot. ♦

ANTHONY TABER, JUNE 6, 1977

"There'd be nothing to it. Put in a computerized guidance system, put in a motor, get rid of the guy with the oar, and you're in business."

"You are to be congratulated on your custard pie."

TOP EVERETT OPIE, JULY 8, 1972   BOTTOM HELEN E. HOKINSON, DECEMBER 30, 1939

"By George, automation does create new jobs!"

ALAN DUNN, MAY 5, 1956

JAMES STEVENSON, AUGUST 19, 1974

BANANA PEELS
BANKS
BARS
BASEBALL
BEACHED WHALES
BEATNIKS
BEDTIME STORIES
BIBLE
BIG FISH LITTLE FISH
BIRD-WATCHERS
BLUEBIRD OF HAPPINESS
BOARDROOMS
BOOKSTORES
BOWLING PIN VS. BALL
BOXING
BUNNIES

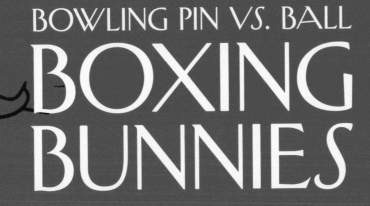

"Forget the banana peel! What we need is a witness."

TOP JACK ZIEGLER, NOVEMBER 11, 2002   BOTTOM JAMES MULLIGAN, NOVEMBER 20, 1965

TOP PETER ARNO, JULY 28, 1962   BOTTOM WARREN MILLER, MAY 27, 1974

SLIP AND FALL

THE PURPOSE OF a banana peel—besides, of course, keeping your banana clean until you're ready to eat it—has been, from time immemorial, a comedic one. Slapstick humor is hardwired into the human brain so fully that even a baby will laugh when its parent pretends to fall (or, much to the chagrin of the parent, when he or she falls for real). It's the original subversion of expectations: A person is walking. Until—*whoops!*— he is not! Hilarious!

It should be clear to even the most casual of observers that the banana peel is the funniest object capable of felling a person. A stuck-out leg is just mean; an oil slick lacks personality. But the banana peel—a bright, happy yellow; a remnant of a recently enjoyed healthful snack—is **the perfect straight man,** cheerfully setting up the joke brought home by the thudding of an unfortunate ass onto the floor. Of course, you can't just draw a man slipping and call it a gag cartoon. For this reason, the cartoonist considers the banana on a more meta level: a joke about a banana peel is a joke about the joke of slipping on a banana peel. For such a lowly scrap, it's awfully think-y. And, God, it's just such a funny word. Banana. *Ba-na-na.* It's nature's perfect joke. ◆

CHARLES ADDAMS, FEBRUARY 25, 1980

JACK ZIEGLER, NOVEMBER 14, 1977

*SEE ALSO CLOWNS, ELVIS, FOOD

B

"That's reality for you."

TOP CHARLES ADDAMS, SEPTEMBER 3, 1979   BOTTOM J.B. HANDELSMAN, MAY 1, 1978

"It's nice to see <u>some</u> people still appreciate the value of a dollar."

"Would you like that all in money?"

TOP EVERETT OPIE, OCTOBER 1, 1973   BOTTOM BRUCE KAPLAN, OCTOBER 29, 2007

*"You're aware, of course, that there's a substantial penalty
for early withdrawal on this account."*

"Throw in one of those brochures about refinancing my home."

TOP TOM CHENEY, MARCH 22, 2004   BOTTOM CAROLITA JOHNSON, MARCH 6, 2006

"*Gee, these new twenties look just
like Monopoly money.*"

"*I don't get paid enough to speak up.*"

"*Can't we talk about something other than money?*"

TOP LEE LORENZ, NOVEMBER 16, 1998   MIDDLE WILLIAM HAEFELI, JUNE 3, 2002   BOTTOM P.C. VEY, MAY 3, 2010

"The usual, Ben."

TOP BILL WOODMAN, MAY 8, 1978   BOTTOM ED ARNO, FEBRUARY 19, 1990

"I'd like to buy everyone a drink. All I ask in return is that you listen patiently to my shallow and simplistic views on a broad range of social and political issues."

"Y'know, I don't know what I'd do without her, but I'd sure like to find out."

TOP J.B. HANDELSMAN, SEPTEMBER 20, 1993 BOTTOM BOB MANKOFF, JUNE 18, 2001

*"You mean you're asking me, John Jenkins, for my
opinion on how to go about fixing all those things up?"*

*"The days of the bartender-psychologist are over,
but I can help if you have any software problems."*

TOP AL ROSS, AUGUST 12, 1972   BOTTOM SIDNEY HARRIS, SEPTEMBER 20, 1999

*"That's my opinion, but before you start actual proceedings
please feel free to consult another bartender."*

WHITNEY DARROW, JR., JANUARY 14, 1961

"Vodka on the rocks, in the rocks, around the rocks, and under the rocks."

"Yes indeed, sir. You strike me as a man who is quite definitely in touch with himself."

"She no longer laughs at my joke."

TOP PETER STEINER, NOVEMBER 17, 2003   MIDDLE J.B. HANDELSMAN, MARCH 7, 1983   BOTTOM PAT BYRNES, NOVEMBER 11, 2002

*"My wife says I need professional help.
You're a pro, aren't you, Ed?"*

"Do you have a Frequent Drinkers card?"

TOP JOSEPH MIRACHI, MARCH 25, 1991   BOTTOM JACK ZIEGLER, MAY 31, 2004

*SEE ALSO COMPLAINT WINDOW, INTOXICATION, PSYCHIATRISTS

"Take my advice, pal. Drink up and get out of here."

"I don't want stock options. I want you to pay your tab."

"Fetch and roll over weren't enough—then they sent me to philosophy classes."

TOP CHARLES BARSOTTI, JULY 13, 1998   MIDDLE CHARLES BARSOTTI, NOVEMBER 1, 1999   BOTTOM CHARLES BARSOTTI, FEBRUARY 14, 2005

"Well executed, both of you!"

"Then we're agreed—it's a great day for a ball game."

TOP MORT GERBERG, OCTOBER 5, 1998   BOTTOM LEE LORENZ, JUNE 2, 2008

"Want to know what I think?"

*"The boos I can handle.
It's the silence of the educated fans that rankles."*

TOP JASON PATTERSON, APRIL 16, 2007   BOTTOM MICHAEL CRAWFORD, MAY 6, 2002

"I'd like you to excel."

*"Don't sweat it.
That's Little League—your dad comes, you choke."*

TOP MIKE TWOHY, APRIL 27, 1987   BOTTOM MICHAEL CRAWFORD, JULY 12, 1999

"Daddy doesn't hate the Yankees.
Daddy has issues with the Yankees."

TOP DAVID SIPRESS, MAY 20, 2002 BOTTOM DANNY SHANAHAN, OCTOBER 10, 2005

"All right! Have it your own way. It was a ball."

TOP BERNARD SCHOENBAUM, AUGUST 12, 1991 BOTTOM BOB MANKOFF, JUNE 9, 1980

"Thou hast eyes to see, and see not!"

PETER ARNO, MAY 10, 1947

"First, let's concentrate on water. Then we'll worry about krill."

"Who ordered the krill pizza?"

TOP SAM GROSS, JUNE 9, 2003   BOTTOM SAM GROSS, SEPTEMBER 5, 2005

"If I were beached, could I do this?"

"Now I remember why I hate the beach."

TOP DANNY SHANAHAN, APRIL 6, 1998 BOTTOM DANNY SHANAHAN, SEPTEMBER 15, 2003

"Damn, he's seen us. Now we'll have to act all compassionate."

"You notice nobody gives a damn about beached minnows."

TOP P.C. VEY, OCTOBER 4, 2010   BOTTOM MICK STEVENS, APRIL 30, 2012

TOP ZACHARY KANIN, JANUARY 28, 2008   BOTTOM ZACHARY KANIN, OCTOBER 20, 2008

"Well, in banking circles I'm considered quite a beatnik."

"Right this way, folks! Here's one!"

TOP ED FISHER, FEBRUARY 18, 1961   BOTTOM BARNEY TOBEY, OCTOBER 1, 1960

*"Frankly, Son, I always hoped that when you finished
school you wouldn't want to join the firm."*

*"It wouldn't work out, Nina. Basically, I suppose,
I want a girl just like the girl who married dear old Dad."*

TOP FRANK MODELL, AUGUST 26, 1961   BOTTOM BARNEY TOBEY, DECEMBER 24, 1960

*"It's kind of you and Martha to offer me a meal while
Erma's away, but, frankly, I'm a little pooped."*

TOP WILLIAM O'BRIAN, JUNE 25, 1960   BOTTOM RICHARD TAYLOR, JULY 22, 1961

"I understand they're secretly married."

WHITNEY DARROW, JR., MAY 14, 1960

"And what's the story behind the story?"

"It's dawn, Dad. Want to knock off for breakfast?"

TOP ARNIE LEVIN, FEBRUARY 8, 1993   BOTTOM MICK STEVENS, NOVEMBER 26, 2001

"Is the Itsy Bitsy Spider obsessive-compulsive?"

*"It's not about the story. It's about Daddy taking time
out of his busy day to read you the story."*

TOP MICHAEL SHAW, FEBRUARY 10, 2003   BOTTOM P.C. VEY, SEPTEMBER 30, 2002

*"Say, Dad, think you could wrap it up?
I have a long day tomorrow."*

*"The little pig with the portfolio of straw and the little pig
with the portfolio of sticks were swallowed up, but the little pig with
the portfolio of bricks withstood the dip in the market."*

TOP BERNARD SCHOENBAUM, NOVEMBER 14, 1994   BOTTOM EDWARD FRASCINO, DECEMBER 15, 1997

*"Remember, in the other version they had a pea-green boat,
and here they're using public transportation."*

"Dad—will the heroine go into rehab?"

TOP MIKE TWOHY, MARCH 29, 1993   BOTTOM EDWARD KOREN, JULY 30, 2007

"I say it's golden, I say it's a calf, and I say worship it!"

*"I'm calling it 'Genesis.'
It's part of a five-book contract."*

TOP STUART LEEDS, OCTOBER 25, 1993   BOTTOM MORT GERBERG, APRIL 13, 1998

"*I really enjoyed the Bible.*"

"*Bring me the head of John the Baptist. Just kidding.
Get me the Paulson file.*"

TOP ROBERT WEBER, DECEMBER 15, 1986   BOTTOM LEO CULLUM, FEBRUARY 26, 1996

"And the Lord spoke to the children of Israel
and said, 'Thou must forswear these practices which
are a blasphemy and an abomination
in my sight, you know what I'm saying?'"

"The Bible... that would be under self-help."

The St. Francis of Assisi Show

TOP LEE LORENZ, JUNE 23, 1997 MIDDLE PETER STEINER, JULY 6, 1998 BOTTOM J.B. HANDELSMAN, OCTOBER 31, 1994

EVE'S MOM

ROZ CHAST, SEPTEMBER 21, 1992

"You mean when I use a phrase like 'Pharaoh <u>dreamed</u> seven cows came up out of the Nile,' or 'God <u>remembered</u> Noah,' or David's wife Michal '<u>despised</u> <u>him</u> <u>in</u> <u>her</u> <u>heart</u>'—that's speculative journalism?"

TOP ED FISHER, SEPTEMBER 20, 1993   BOTTOM ARNIE LEVIN, JANUARY 20, 1997

*SEE ALSO ADAM & EVE, HEAVEN, NOAH'S ARK

B

"Having completed the formation of the earth, on the seventh day the Lord rested. Then, on the eight day, the Lord said, 'Let there be problems.' And <u>there</u> <u>were</u> <u>problems.</u>"

TOP JACK ZIEGLER, JULY 12, 1993 BOTTOM DANA FRADON, OCTOBER 18, 1993

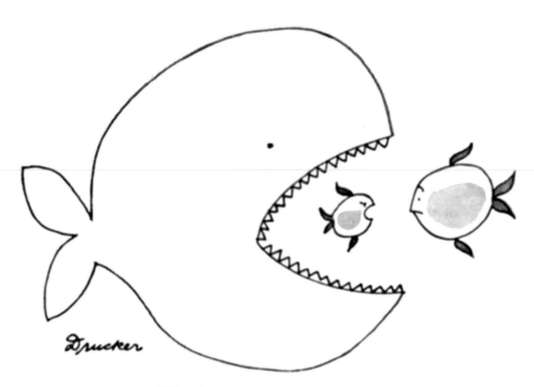

"When I want your advice, I'll ask for it."

TOP BORIS DRUCKER, AUGUST 17, 1968   BOTTOM JOHN O'BRIEN, OCTOBER 28, 1991

TOP JACK ZIEGLER, JULY 16, 2001   BOTTOM DANNY SHANAHAN, JUNE 28, 2010

TOP ROBERT KRAUS, APRIL 30, 1960   BOTTOM DEAN VIETOR, AUGUST 16, 1976

TOP SAM GROSS, NOVEMBER 6, 2006   BOTTOM BOB MANKOFF, FEBRUARY 9, 1981

"Maybe it doesn't want to be identified."

"This is my only New York appearance this year."

TOP LIAM WALSH, JANUARY 9, 2017   BOTTOM EDWARD KOREN, SEPTEMBER 17, 1979

"Shall I sing like the wild Atlantic canary or the
domesticated yellow canary?"

TOP MISCHA RICHTER, SEPTEMBER 29, 1956   BOTTOM BENJAMIN SCHWARTZ, SEPTEMBER 10, 2012

"I'll be damned—a Bachman's warbler on the President's limo!"

TOP C. COVERT DARBYSHIRE, JULY 2, 2001 BOTTOM FRANK MODELL, JULY 23, 1960

TOP MISCHA RICHTER, AUGUST 20, 1979 BOTTOM WARREN MILLER, JANUARY 24, 1970

"Hi! I'm the Bluebird of Happiness.
Can I get your ex-wife's new address?"

"Hi, Billy. I'm the Bluebird of Happiness.
I would have been here sooner, but I've had obligations."

TOP DANNY SHANAHAN, APRIL 15, 1996   BOTTOM JAMES STEVENSON, AUGUST 4, 1975

*"Happiness is not readily transmittable
from bluebirds to humans."*

"The Bluebird of Happiness is on his way. We're security."

TOP FRANK COTHAM, MAY 15, 2006   BOTTOM MIKE TWOHY, APRIL 27, 1998

"*Hi! I'm the Bluebird of Quiet Resignation.*"

TOP ROZ CHAST, APRIL 25, 2011 BOTTOM DAVID CHRISTIANSON, APRIL 12, 1976

"Hiya, hiya, hiya, guy. I'm the Bluebird of Prozac."

"Hi! I'm the Bluebird of Death."

TOP BOB MANKOFF, AUGUST 9, 1993   BOTTOM DAVID SIPRESS, MAY 25, 2005

"If there's no more old business and no more
new business, let's declare bankruptcy."

"And now at this point in the meeting I'd like to shift
the blame away from me and onto someone else."

TOP MIKE TWOHY, OCTOBER 22, 2001 BOTTOM MICHAEL MASLIN, SEPTEMBER 16, 1985

*"This is goodbye, gentlemen. I have met another
board of directors, and we have fallen in love."*

*"The figures for the last quarter are in. We made
significant gains in the fifteen-to-twenty-six-year-old
age group, but we lost our immortal souls."*

TOP SIDNEY HARRIS, APRIL 7, 1997   BOTTOM WARREN MILLER, FEBRUARY 14, 1994

"And, while there's no reason yet to panic,
I think it only prudent that we make preparations to panic."

"Obviously, some people here do not appreciate
the gravity of our situation."

TOP BOB MANKOFF, DECEMBER 16, 1996   BOTTOM FRANK MODELL, OCTOBER 14, 1985

"We realize it's a win-win, Jenkins—we're trying to figure out a way to make it a win-lose."

"For God's sake, Edwards. Put the laser pointer away."

TOP MATTHEW DIFFEE, NOVEMBER 14, 2011   BOTTOM LEO CULLUM, FEBRUARY 1, 1999

TOP PETER STEINER, DECEMBER 22, 1997   BOTTOM BERNARD SCHOENBAUM, SEPTEMBER 19, 1994

"It's not in stock, but I can have it written."

TOP PAUL KARASIK, ARPIL 14, 2008   BOTTOM DANNY SHANAHAN, AUGUST 14, 1995

"*Look, Mother, this section should interest you.*"

"*No caffè latte? And you call yourselves a bookstore?*"

TOP DAVID SIPRESS, NOVEMBER 12, 2001   BOTTOM DANNY SHANAHAN, JUNE 27, 1994

"*I like novels where the protagonist is a thinly veiled version of me.*"

TOP WILLIAM HAEFELI, OCTOBER 20, 2008   BOTTOM BARBARA SMALLER, MARCH 15, 2010

"Payback time."

TOP ZACHARY KANIN, MARCH 26, 2012   BOTTOM FARLEY KATZ, NOVEMBER 23, 2009

TOP PETER MUELLER, MAY 2, 2005   BOTTOM CHARLES ADDAMS, JUNE 16, 1962

"Don't say it—I'll clean out my desk."

"Have you ever considered another line of work?"

TOP CHARLES BARSOTTI, MARCH 24, 2003   MIDDLE CHARLES BARSOTTI, MAY 13, 2002   BOTTOM CHARLES BARSOTTI, JANUARY 27, 1975

Kanin

The Evolution of Bowling

TOP ZACHARY KANIN, MARCH 22, 2010   BOTTOM MICK STEVENS, MARCH 23, 2009

"And no hitting below where a normal person wears his belt."

"Watch out for his right hook."

TOP ZACHARY KANIN, MAY 16, 2011   BOTTOM BOB MANKOFF, MARCH 17, 2014

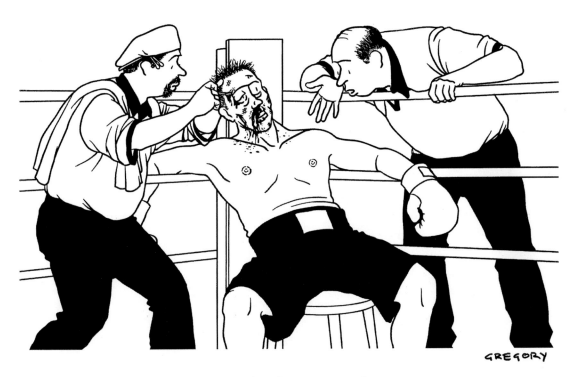

"Sure, he's pulverizing your face,
but you're chipping away at his likability."

"Hang in there. If you win this bout,
you get to fight his mother."

TOP ALEX GREGORY, MARCH 29, 2006   BOTTOM KIM WARP, DECEMBER 21, 2009

ELDON DEDINI, SEPTEMBER 28, 1957

SCHOOL OF HARD KNOCKS

YOU WILL BE HIT. That's life. At times you will be bloodied, on the ropes, or even knocked down. Cartoonists have never had to look far to find the right metaphor for taking it on the chin. During the early decades of gag cartooning, boxing was a regular event on the radio and, later, on television. People could relate to the fighter getting this helpful reminder from his coach: "And remember, kid, you've got Blue Cross." **Humor softened the real-life blows.** As boxing faded from its old glory, cartoons began to explore subtler ways to get hit, as with the female boxer "weighing in at five pounds more than she'd like." Spouses found one another waiting for them in the ring. Or the effects of aging were recognized as a low blow. The metaphor keeps working in ever more cunning ways, seeking out more soft spots, as if the cartoonist were circling us, probing for a new angle, toying with us to let our guard down and then—*bam!*—land a punch line. ♦

*"Your mother wanted you to have this for good luck.
It's her foot."*

THE PHANTOM OF THE GARDEN

TOP HARRY BLISS, SEPTEMBER 11, 2000   BOTTOM CHARLES BARSOTTI, FEBRUARY 15, 1988

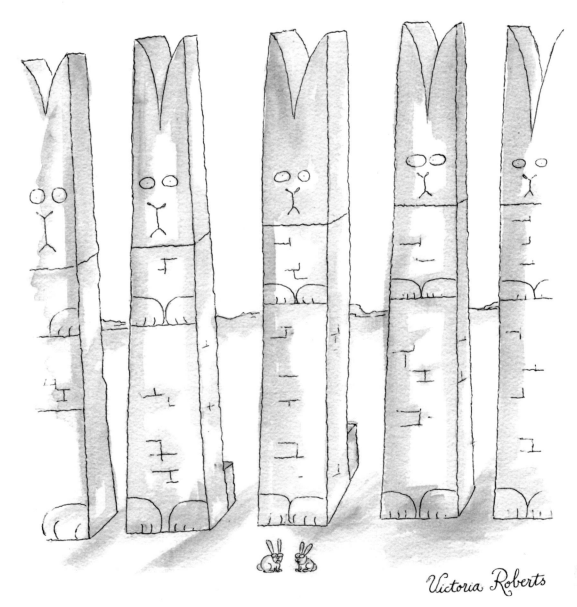

Victoria Roberts

"*We were once a great civilization.*"

"*Anyone here named Hippity?*"

TOP VICTORIA ROBERTS, AUGUST 16, 2010   BOTTOM CHARLES BARSOTTI, APRIL 10, 2000

SAM GROSS, FEBRUARY 2, 1976

*SEE ALSO EASTER BUNNY, MAGICIANS, TORTOISE & THE HARE

B

*"I think you have the pinkest eyes, the cutest nose,
and the fluffiest little white tail in all the world."*

"You are one sick rabbit."

TOP LEE LORENZ, JULY 1, 1967   BOTTOM SAM GROSS, SEPTEMBER 14, 2009

CARS
CAT VS. MOUSE
CAVEMEN & -WOMEN
CELL PHONES
CENSORSHIP
CENTAURS
CHRISTOPHER COLUMBUS
CINDERELLA
CLASSICAL MUSIC
CLOWNS
COMMUTERS
COMPLAINT WINDOW
COMPUTERS
COOKING
COWBOYS
CRASH TEST DUMMIES
CRIME SCENES
CROSSWORDS

"*Haven't you something more immense?*"

DONALD REILLY, JUNE 17, 1996

*"Sure, it has some life left in it, but you might
ask yourself just what kind of life it would be."*

TOP MICHAEL MASLIN, DECEMBER 12, 1994   BOTTOM ROZ CHAST, DECEMBER 9, 1996

"Your car will be right down, Mr. Lundquist."

"We'll work with you—
if cash is a problem, come back when it isn't."

TOP GEORGE BOOTH, AUGUST 17, 1981   BOTTOM ERIC TEITELBAUM, SEPTEMBER 19, 1994

"Often, it's sullen and withdrawn, and then,
suddenly, it becomes hostile and vengeful."

"Do I know how fast I was going? Isn't that your job?"

TOP EDWARD KOREN, APRIL 19, 1993   BOTTOM HARRY BLISS, OCTOBER 2, 2006

*"We located the hissing noise, Mr. Watkins.
Your wife's mother is in the back seat."*

"It will be your job to create major delays."

TOP GEORGE BOOTH, NOVEMBER 13, 1978   BOTTOM FRANK COTHAM, APRIL 18, 2005

*"If I take back what I said about your pants,
will you let me go?"*

"Hey, is this great traffic, or what?"

TOP HARRY BLISS, SEPTEMBER 14, 1998   BOTTOM BOB MANKOFF, JULY 6, 1987

"For God's sake, think!
Why is he being so nice to you?"

TOP BERNARD SCHOENBAUM, NOVEMBER 2, 1992   BOTTOM SAM GROSS, SEPTEMBER 7, 1998

"Badges? We don't have to show you no stinkin' badges!"

"Sam is very focused."

TOP J.C. DUFFY, FEBRUARY 18, 2002 BOTTOM EDWARD KOREN, JULY 7, 1997

"The system sucks."

TOP BRUCE KAPLAN, MAY 23, 1994   BOTTOM MICK STEVENS, MAY 31, 1999

*SEE ALSO DOGS VS. CATS, KITTENS, LION TAMERS

"Do you have a reservation?"

TOP ERIC LEWIS, APRIL 7, 2008   BOTTOM SAM GROSS, APRIL 27, 1998

"I've had to be both hunter and gatherer."

*"When I was your age, things were exactly
the way they are now."*

TOP TOM CHENEY, SEPTEMBER 22, 1997 BOTTOM ROBERT LEIGHTON, APRIL 25, 2011

*"Did you remember to scatter a few lance points and
arrowheads back there for future generations to ponder?"*

TOP KIM WARP, JUNE 14, 2010   BOTTOM JACK ZIEGLER, MARCH 24, 2008

C

BACK TO THE STONE AGE

C AVEMEN: THEY'RE JUST like us! Except dumber, hairier, and handier with a spear. We make fun of their brutish ways, their simple minds, their penchant for animal-print singlets, but we're really making fun of ourselves—our ur-selves, our pure selves. Reaching back to the dawn of human existence gives the gag writer a useful shorthand for the human condition: **'twas always thus, even in caveman days.** We delight in transposing our modern foibles onto their Paleolithic milieu because it gives us a new (if very old) perspective on the world. And, really, on some level, isn't it comforting to imagine our cave ancestors engaging in petty décor one-upmanship after a long day of chasing a mammoth? One hates to imagine that our forebears were just humorless survivalists.

Also, they're the one group of people you don't have to worry about pissing off with your joke. ♦

"Now what?"

PATTERSON

JASON PATTERSON, SEPTEMBER 17, 2007

*"There—now I've taught you everything
I know about splitting rocks."*

"They're all Neanderthals."

TOP GAHAN WILSON, APRIL 9, 2007 BOTTOM DANNY SHANAHAN, NOVEMBER 24, 2014

"He's done it all. There's nothing left to draw."

"We'll start out by speaking in simple declarative sentences."

TOP TOM TORO, SEPTEMBER 2, 2013   BOTTOM FRANK COTHAM, MAY 28, 2007

"I'm putting you on speaker—it's essential for
everyone to hear our conversation."

TOP LIAM WALSH, AUGUST 5, 2013   BOTTOM TOM CHITTY, APRIL 18, 2016

"Keep your eyes peeled for a place to
charge our phones, men."

TOP TIM HAMILTON, JUNE 22, 2015   BOTTOM DAN ROE, JUNE 1, 2015

"You still working on charging that phone?"

"Oh, sorry—I think I just butt-summoned you."

TOP DREW DERNAVICH, MARCH 31, 2014   BOTTOM JOE DATOR, MAY 18, 2015

"I only keep selfies where I'm unrecognizably attractive."

TOP LIANA FINCK, AUGUST 10, 2015   BOTTOM WILLIAM HAEFELI, MAY 4, 2015

"No smut!"

*"Have you noticed? Fewer people go
'Tsk, tsk' these days."*

TOP WILLIAM STEIG, SEPTEMBER 5, 1964   BOTTOM WARREN MILLER, APRIL 17, 1971

"Sometimes I just want to curl up with
a good book and burn it."

"Mischa! You're really asking
for a midnight knock on the door!"

TOP ZACHARY KANIN, AUGUST 2, 2010 BOTTOM BARNEY TOBEY, JULY 13, 1963

YOU CAN'T SAY THAT

CARTOONISTS DO NOT live on desert islands. They spend little time in corporate boardrooms and rarely see the actual Grim Reaper. But there is at least one cartoon trope that casts a shadow over their everyday lives: censorship.

Cartoons are drawn for publication. Publications can be censored. And cartoonists know this all too well. Although they may think that censors should ███████████ their ████████████████ in the ██████████████████, such venting hardly dispels their anxieties about being silenced, suppressed, redacted, or whitelisted.

Censorship gets a lot of press. We demand it, and we condemn it. When does free speech become hate speech? And who gets to decide? These matters are particularly prickly in the realm of humor. Many cartoons **teeter on the edge between exposing a truth and giving offense.** For some of them, that shaky balance is the whole point.

Michael Shaw takes this one step further—into oblivion. If you can't say something nice, after all, or, more properly, if you're not allowed to say anything that's not nice, there's really nothing for a cartoonist to say. Where to draw the line between tasteless and truthful? Exactly where cartoonists are drawing it. ♦

PLEASE ENJOY THIS CULTURALLY, ETHNICALLY, RELIGIOUSLY, AND POLITICALLY CORRECT CARTOON RESPONSIBLY. THANK YOU.

SHAW

MICHAEL SHAW, FEBRUARY 27, 2006

"And, of course, we don't want to offend any majority groups, either."

WHITNEY DARROW, JR., MARCH 11, 1950

"If it turns me on, it's smut."

PORTIONS OF
THE COMING
DAY MAY BE
OFFENSIVE
TO SOME.
PARTICIPANT
DISCRETION
ADVISED.

"It seems to me that you people
could use a few X and R ratings!"

TOP HERBERT GOLDBERG, NOVEMBER 4, 1972   MIDDLE CHARLES BARSOTTI, DECEMBER 15, 1975   BOTTOM BARNEY TOBEY, JANUARY 23, 1971

"I'm worried about Nick. His horse came back without him."

TOP WILLIAM O'BRIAN, NOVEMBER 30, 1957   BOTTOM FRANK MODELL, MARCH 2, 1963

"Derek and I have always been very aware of the nutritional value of whole grains."

TOP DANNY SHANAHAN, OCTOBER 30, 1989   BOTTOM WARREN MILLER, SEPTEMBER 24, 1990

"*It happens that neither of us is interested.*"

"*It's not a fit night out for man nor beast.*"

TOP J.B. HANDELSMAN, OCTOBER 17, 1970   BOTTOM ANATOL KOVARSKY, JULY 10, 1954

"I just _saw_ a vet, and he told me to see you."

"The left rear has nice eyes."

TOP FRANK MODELL, SEPTEMBER 12, 1959 BOTTOM WARREN MILLER, JANUARY 14, 1991

"All I can say is thank goodness for teleconferencing."

"Tired? Bored? Part man, part horse?
Here's an amazing new product designed just for you."

TOP PETER STEINER, DECEMBER 17, 2001   BOTTOM MICHAEL MASLIN, JANUARY 6, 2006

*"Being a hybrid, I get to have my way with a variety of species,
and at the same time I enjoy a healthy tax credit."*

*"She turned out to be my kind of horse
but not my kind of woman."*

TOP JACK ZIEGLER, SEPTEMBER 3, 2001 BOTTOM DONALD REILLY, MARCH 13, 2000

"In fourteen hundred and ninety-two, you will sail the ocean blue."

TOP MICK STEVENS, APRIL 29, 1991   BOTTOM AL ROSS, SEPTEMBER 11, 1971

"We have decided to finance your voyage,
Mr. Columbus, even though we are disappointed that
you failed to produce your high-school transcripts."

"Just tell me about the new continent.
I don't give a damn what you've discovered about yourself."

TOP J.B. HANDELSMAN, OCTOBER 13, 1997   BOTTOM BRUCE KAPLAN, OCTOBER 18, 1999

*"Well, for the love of God! You're supposed to be on
the Santa Maria waving goodbye."*

RICHARD DECKER, SEPTEMBER 14, 1935

CHRISTOPHER COLUMBUS, SEEKING VEGETABLE OIL, DISCOVERS SUNFLOWER OIL INSTEAD.

"Your Majesty, my voyage will not only forge a new route to the spices of the East but also create over three thousand new jobs."

TOP MICHAEL MASLIN, NOVEMBER 5, 1990   BOTTOM DANA FRADON, OCTOBER 19, 1992

"She wears glass slippers? This kind of aggravation I don't need."

"Would you mind stepping out of the pumpkin, please?"

TOP ROBERT LEIGHTON, FEBRUARY 14, 2005   BOTTOM MICHAEL MASLIN, OCTOBER 18, 1999

"*O.K., let's try this again.*"

"*If the coach and horses and the footmen and the beautiful
clothes all turned back into the pumpkin and the mice and the rags,
then how come the glass slipper didn't turn back, too?*"

TOP ZACHARY KANIN, SEPTEMBER 8, 2008   BOTTOM HENRY MARTIN, MARCH 11, 1974

"How the hell do I know if it's organic?
Do you want a coach or don't you?"

"I'll call you back. I'm in the middle of a make-over."

TOP LEE LORENZ, FEBRUARY 26, 1972 MIDDLE WARREN MILLER, DECEMBER 13, 1993 BOTTOM SAM GROSS, MARCH 19, 2001

*"If you think I've changed,
you ought to get a good look at yourself!"*

WILLIAM O'BRIAN, MAY 14, 1960

"Look, honey, the glass slipper still fits."

TOP JOHN O'BRIEN, NOVEMBER 18, 1991   BOTTOM EDWARD FRASCINO, MAY 21, 1990

*SEE ALSO GOLDILOCKS, HANSEL & GRETEL, RAPUNZEL

*"I like 'Cinderella'— it's just that I feel the characters
of the stepsisters are underwritten."*

TOP ARNIE LEVIN, NOVEMBER 22, 1993   BOTTOM BARBARA SMALLER, JUNE 11, 2007

*"We will begin with Schubert's
'Unfinished' Symphony, and that will be followed by
Beethoven's 'Unwanted Sexual' Overture."*

"On the other hand, it's been a great year for Berlioz."

TOP J.B. HANDELSMAN, NOVEMBER 23, 1998   BOTTOM LEE LORENZ, JUNE 2, 2003

"Can't you just say 'Scarlatti' instead of 'Scarlatti, of course'?"

THE JUILLIARD AIR QUARTET

TOP WILLIAM HAMILTON, MARCH 17, 1973   BOTTOM JACK ZIEGLER, OCTOBER 21, 1985

"String quartets! Minor rhapsodies! Little symphonies!"

TOP MICK STEVENS, AUGUST 17, 1981   BOTTOM JACK ZIEGLER, MARCH 29, 1999

"Did I say Henny Youngman? I meant to say Sergei Prokofiev."

*"In a moment we'll have a few words by the chairman of the board.
But, first, Mahler's Eighth Symphony."*

TOP ROBERT WEBER, JUNE 9, 2003   BOTTOM MISCHA RICHTER, MARCH 10, 1980

"Make 'em laugh."

"I've heard a lot about you—all nutty, of course."

TOP MICHAEL MASLIN, JUNE 8, 2009   BOTTOM CHARLES BARSOTTI, FEBRUARY 13, 1995

"A funny thing happened at work today."

"I think we're in luck!"

TOP DANNY SHANAHAN, NOVEMBER 19, 2001   BOTTOM GAHAN WILSON, SEPTEMBER 6, 2010

"Just even it out."

TOP SAM GROSS, NOVEMBER 6, 2006   BOTTOM DANNY SHANAHAN, JULY 1, 2002

"I tell the truth, and sometimes it's funny."

TOP SAM GROSS, OCTOBER 22, 2007   BOTTOM P.C. VEY, AUGUST 6, 2007

"Now that I've been let go, the commute is all I have."

"Walter had an attack of road rage in the driveway."

TOP P.C. VEY, JANUARY 6, 2003   BOTTOM GEORGE BOOTH, DECEMBER 15, 1997

THE 8:17 FROM DOBBS FERRY

"Valhalla."

TOP STUART LEEDS, JULY 11, 1988   BOTTOM WARREN MILLER, SEPTEMBER 28, 1987

"Of course, on casual Fridays I'm the fifties Elvis."

OLD COMMUTERS' HOME

TOP DANNY SHANAHAN, MARCH 30, 1998   BOTTOM MICK STEVENS, SEPTEMBER 2, 1985

*"This next blues is about the 5:37 to Scarsdale, and
how it's frequently late, and crowded."*

TOP SIDNEY HARRIS, MAY 17, 1999   BOTTOM J.C. DUFFY, JANUARY 20, 2003

*"Look, I'm not denying the validity of your grievances.
I just think they'd be better addressed at home, Helen."*

TOP WARREN MILLER, APRIL 15, 1974   BOTTOM BOB MANKOFF, MAY 16, 2005

"*Young man, I was complaining about things in this store before you were born!*"

"*Aside from the toaster, how's life been treating you?*"

"*I think I speak for all of us.*"

TOP LEFT PETER ARNO, AUGUST 5, 1961 TOP RIGHT PETER ARNO, MAY 22, 1965 BOTTOM ZACHARY KANIN, JANUARY 14, 2008

"Complaints? Sixth floor—for all the good it'll do you."

TOP ROBERT WEBER, DECEMBER 9, 1991 BOTTOM FRANK MODELL, JANUARY 18, 1969

"Now, don't you start complaining."

"It's fancy-schmantzy. I just wanted fancy."

TOP FRANK MODELL, JANUARY 3, 1977   BOTTOM ARNIE LEVIN, JANUARY 11, 1993

"I'll be damned. It says, 'Cogito, ergo sum.'"

"Is it fair to make it compute a way to make a better computer?"

TOP MISCHA RICHTER, NOVEMBER 1, 1958   BOTTOM ALAN DUNN, DECEMBER 20, 1958

"We've called you here today to announce that, according to our computer, by the year 2000 everything is going to be peachy."

TOP LEE LORENZ, APRIL 14, 1973   BOTTOM AL ROSS, OCTOBER 3, 1964

"Miss Johnson, this machine
always forgets to carry the one."

"If they ever develop a computer
that can bow and scrape, we've had it."

TOP HENRY MARTIN, NOVEMBER 2, 1968   MIDDLE KENNETH MAHOOD, MAY 23, 1970   BOTTOM WILLIAM HAMILTON, MAY 22, 1965

CHARLES ADDAMS, JANUARY 21, 1967

"The problem is 'The Effect of Automation on
Unemployment in the Next Decade.' See if you can solve that!"

ALAN DUNN, MAY 5, 1962

*SEE ALSO AUTOMATION, INTERNET, LABOR VS. MANAGEMENT

"Damn you, Winkle, did you have to go and ask it which came first— the chicken or the egg?"

"Well, dear, how did all your electronic brains work today?"

TOP DANA FRADON, AUGUST 28, 1971   MIDDLE STAN HUNT, JULY 28, 1962   BOTTOM LEE LORENZ, APRIL 12, 1969

"They're marinated in hot water for six hours."

"Yo—I'm way overdone in here!"

TOP LEO CULLUM, JUNE 4, 2007   BOTTOM GAHAN WILSON, DECEMBER 24, 2007

"If it says to add water, and I'm the one who adds it, I'm cooking."

"Actually, he's not so bad, considering that he's recipe-dependent."

TOP BARBARA SMALLER, JULY 30, 2001   BOTTOM MORT GERBERG, AUGUST 10, 1992

"So this is where the magic happens."

"Hello? Risotto-crisis hot line?"

TOP ROBERT WEBER, JANUARY 26, 2004 BOTTOM LIZA DONNELLY, APRIL 12, 1999

TOO MANY LAWYERS SPOIL THE BROTH

ROZ CHAST, MAY 21, 2007

"That there's one bowlegged cowboy."

"Take this, Luke. They say it's impossible to get a
decent baguette west of the Pecos."

TOP TOM TORO, AUGUST 9, 2010   BOTTOM LEO CULLUM, DECEMBER 10, 2001

"All hat and no cattle but, my god, what a hat."

"O.K., fellers, we shoot first, then Q. and A."

TOP CHARLES BARSOTTI, FEBRUARY 9, 2009   BOTTOM MATTHEW DIFFEE, JUNE 26, 2006

"You ain't from around here, are you, Mister?"

*"That's the last time he'll disseminate
disparaging remarks and slanderous disinformation
through out-of-context misquoting in this town."*

TOP JACK ZIEGLER, OCTOBER 22, 2007   BOTTOM TOM CHENEY, APRIL 6, 2009

*"Hell, I'm just saying it would be nice if
someone would play percussion for once."*

TOP JACK ZIEGLER, AUGUST 19, 1991   BOTTOM CHRISTOPHER WEYANT, APRIL 8, 2002

"Well, I'd better go now. I'm almost at the wall."

"Seat belts unfastened? Excellent."

TOP DAVE COVERLY, APRIL 23, 2007   BOTTOM JACK ZIEGLER, MARCH 9, 2015

TOP STUART LEEDS, SEPTEMBER 11, 1995   BOTTOM BERNARD SCHOENBAUM, FEBRUARY 21, 1994

"Ma'am, it's your husband. There's been an auto accident."

TOP ARNIE LEVIN, AUGUST 16, 1993

"You were an accident."

TOP SAM GROSS, MAY 22, 1995   MIDDLE DAVID SIPRESS, JULY 10, 2006   BOTTOM JACK ZIEGLER, DECEMBER 5, 1994

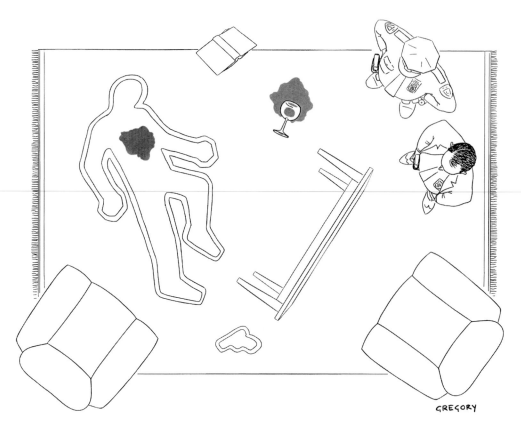

"Notice how the rug really ties the crime scene together."

"Any clues?"

TOP ALEX GREGORY, NOVEMBER 19, 2001   BOTTOM SHANNON WHEELER, JANUARY 30, 2012

"Don't you hate it when you plant evidence but forget where?"

"The killer had to be a man.
Not only is the knife still bloody—it wasn't even put in the sink."

"…or, for those of us who don't speak French,
'Look for the woman.'"

"So, did you hear about all the excitement?"

TOP ROBERT KRAUS, FEBRUARY 18, 1956   BOTTOM GAHAN WILSON, JANUARY 10, 1994

"Nope. Looks to me like a clear-cut case of suicide by
somehow reaching around behind the back and sticking
a knife in backward. Let's get a drink."

"Sure, Liz, come on up for a drink! And don't mind
the place—it's a bit of a crime scene right now."

TOP ZACHARY KANIN, DECEMBER 22, 2008   BOTTOM MICHAEL CRAWFORD, JANUARY 27, 2014

"And this is a crossword puzzle I'm working on."

TOP DREW DERNAVICH, NOVEMBER 29, 2010   BOTTOM BOB MANKOFF, JANUARY 12, 2004

"New York 'Times,' Saturday crossword, 1999,
twenty-two minutes, ballpoint."

BEFORE

AFTER

TOP JULIA SUITS, OCTOBER 1, 2012   BOTTOM JACK ZIEGLER, AUGUST 17, 1987

"29 Across is classified, too, sir. They're all classified."

"I really don't see how giving you a six-letter
word for a sixteenth-century
crested metal helmet helps my problem."

TOP P.C. VEY, APRIL 13, 2015   BOTTOM J.C. DUFFY, JULY 26, 1999

"Good news—a four-letter word for 'earthen pot' is 'olla.'"

TOP ARNIE LEVIN, NOVEMBER 24, 1975   BOTTOM DANNY SHANAHAN, MAY 29, 2000

DANCE
DATING
DENTISTRY
DEPRESSION
DESERT ISLAND
DIET
DIVORCE
DOCTOR VS. PATIENT
DOGS VS. CATS
DOOMSAYERS
DREAMS
DUELS

"I'd suggest you keep them away from the gingerbread men."

TOP ROZ CHAST, SEPTEMBER 11, 2006   BOTTOM GAHAN WILSON, DECEMBER 1, 2008

"You've either got it or you haven't got it."

WHITNEY DARROW, JR., MAY 13, 1961

THE CHOREOGRAPH

TOP JACK ZIEGLER, JANUARY 20, 2003 BOTTOM BRUCE PETTY, FEBRUARY 27, 1965

*"Say what's on your mind, Harris—
the language of dance has always eluded me."*

"Walk, hell—I gotta dance!"

TOP BOB MANKOFF, JANUARY 14, 1991   BOTTOM DANNY SHANAHAN, MARCH 31, 2003

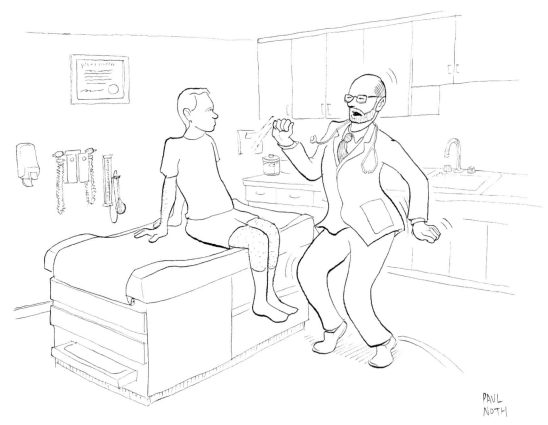

"Do you find it painful when I get funky?"

TOP MATTHEW DIFFEE, JUNE 14, 1999   BOTTOM PAUL NOTH, AUGUST 11, 2008

*SEE ALSO ELVIS, MUSIC

D

"Our purpose in this dance is to suggest an irrigation system that has just been completed and that will make the entire valley fertile."

"If that's 'Dancing with the Stars,' we only work as a group."

TOP RICHARD TAYLOR, DECEMBER 13, 1947 BOTTOM CHARLES BARSOTTI, JANUARY 23, 2006

"Yes, Doreen, I think I <u>am</u> capable of unconditional love."

"After we have sex but before I kill you,
I'm going to need your help with some shelves."

"Why am I talking this loud? Because I'm wrong."

*"Katia, I know that with the right combination of therapy
and medication I could have a committed relationship with you."*

TOP RICHARD CLINE, AUGUST 4, 1986   BOTTOM EDWARD KOREN, APRIL 3, 1995

"*They're a perfect match—she's high-maintenance, and he can fix anything.*"

"*Since we're both being honest, I should tell you I have fleas.*"

TOP EDWARD KOREN, APRIL 8, 1996   BOTTOM BRUCE KAPLAN, JANUARY 23, 1995

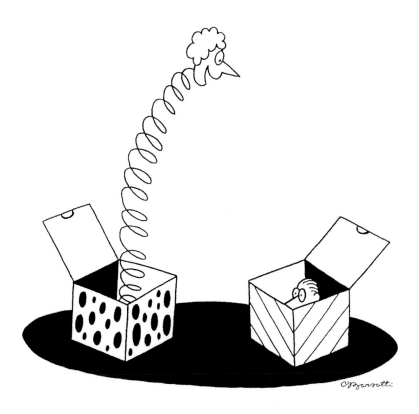

"Come __on__, Louis. No risk, no reward."

*"Don't you understand? I love you! I need you!
I want to spend the rest of my vacation with you!"*

TOP CHARLES BARSOTTI, AUGUST 3, 1992   BOTTOM MIKE TWOHY, JUNE 16, 1997

"*I had a nice time, Steve.
Would you like to come in, settle down,
and raise a family?*"

B. Smaller

"*I'm not saying that I don't
have intimacy issues. I'm just saying that
I prefer to work on them by myself.*"

"*Do you mind if I say something helpful
about your personality?*"

TOP BOB MANKOFF, FEBRUARY 8, 1999   MIDDLE BARBARA SMALLER, DECEMBER 7, 1998   BOTTOM ROBERT WEBER, AUGUST 4, 1997

*SEE ALSO CAVEMEN & WOMEN

D

"The thing I like about New York, Claudia, is you."

ROBERT WEBER, JULY 2, 1984

"Of course, the money's good, but it's the teeth that keep me coming back."

"Me? I'm not in a dental plan. I thought you were in a dental plan."

TOP PETER STEINER, JULY 31, 1995 BOTTOM J.B. HANDELSMAN, OCTOBER 19, 1981

"We have adult teeth now, Debbie, and, as such, they demand adult pain."

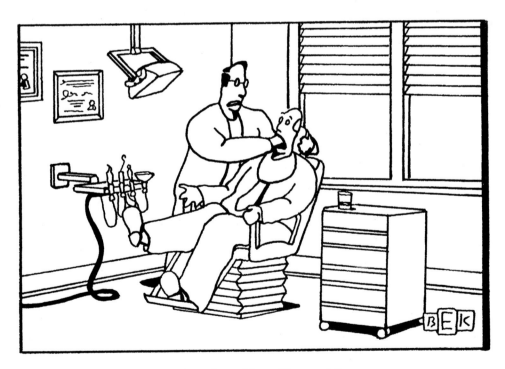

"Gee, this is like pulling teeth."

TOP JACK ZIEGLER, DECEMBER 3, 2001   BOTTOM BRUCE KAPLAN, APRIL 5, 1993

THE DRILL AND THE FLOSS

TEETH ARE TROUBLE. They're trouble on arrival and on departure—trouble when they erupt in the mouths of infants ("teething pain"), and when they withdraw from the mouths of the elderly. They're trouble in between. (As a Ziegler dentist tells a patient, "We have adult teeth now and, as such, they demand adult pain.") Dentists, accordingly, are ambiguous figures who cause us pain to spare us pain; we regard them, variously, with mistrust and gratitude. Cartoonists have recognized the possibilities. They know that the basic office tableau—the chair, the drill, the bared dentition—means one thing from the perspective of the dentist with the difficult patient, and another thing from the perspective of the patient with a difficult dentist. They wonder how the world looks to the expert who notices the teeth before the smile. They wonder whether they would have made a better living if they had given up their pens for those drills. Still, there's more than one way to provide relief by inducing discomfort. And cartoonists, being observant souls, have taken instruction from the clinic: **Bite down. ♦**

"*I detect a little laxity in your flossing.*"

EDWARD KOREN, DECEMBER 9, 1991

"And dentistry? I've heard dentistry has its rewards also."

"Cosmetic dentistry changed my life."

TOP JACK ZIEGLER, JUNE 10, 1974   BOTTOM PETER STEINER, NOVEMBER 9, 1992

"It's your dentist, Charlie. He says it's been five years!"

"Sharon, if we can fit another mirror in there
it will look like his teeth go on forever."

TOP AL ROSS, FEBRUARY 23, 1987   BOTTOM ZACHARY KANIN, APRIL 5, 2010

"It's a new anti-depressant—instead of swallowing it,
you throw it at anyone who appears to be having a good time."

"Yes, I'm somewhat depressed,
but seasonally adjusted I'm probably happy enough."

TOP TOM CHENEY, JULY 2, 2001   BOTTOM BOB MANKOFF, DECEMBER 10, 1984

"Now that I've swung back to depression,
I'm truly sorry for what I did when I was manic."

"Ah! Here it is!"

TOP J.B. HANDELSMAN, AUGUST 24, 1992   BOTTOM MICHAEL CRAWFORD, AUGUST 23, 1999

SIPRESS

"This next one is a sad little blues tune about love and pain that I wrote before I started taking Celexa."

"What's the next best medicine?"

S.GROSS

TOP DAVID SIPRESS, OCTOBER 9, 2000   MIDDLE CHARLES BARSOTTI, JANUARY 9, 1995   BOTTOM SAM GROSS, SEPTEMBER 1, 1980

*SEE ALSO FUNERALS, HAPPINESS, PSYCHIATRISTS

"*More lithium.*"

TOM CHENEY, DECEMBER 6, 1993

"My entire family's coming for the holidays."

TOP DAVID SIPRESS, DECEMBER 16, 2002   BOTTOM BOB MANKOFF, OCTOBER 13, 1980

D

"Would it kill you to compost?"

"Great party last night."

TOP DANNY SHANAHAN, OCTOBER 15, 2001   BOTTOM SAM MEANS, MARCH 14, 2005

TOTALLY WRECKED

T HE DESERT-ISLAND CARTOON arose out of desert-island literature, epitomized by "Robinson Crusoe." Three centuries ago, shipwrecks were common, and people really did get stranded, sometimes even on desert islands. The cartoon genre began, though, when the hazard had become merely imaginary. It's the classic **"tragedy plus time equals comedy"** effect. At *The New Yorker,* these cartoons made their appearance in the nineteen-thirties, and in these older versions, the desert island is quite large, and a ship is sinking in the background. There's a signaled narrative: you understand how the castaways got on the island. Later, the island became an icon—not an island, but the idea of one—the classic tiny lobe of land with a single palm tree. The genre shifted in thematic ways, too. The early cartoons were generally about being removed from the social strictures of the time. In the nineteen-thirties or forties, if a man and a woman were on an island, the joke probably had a sexual spin. Later, the drawings typically represented isolation, not liberation. Eventually, the trope became self-conscious to the point of self-referentiality: the subject of a desert-island cartoon might be desert-island cartoons. "No man is an island," a stranded man reflects in one from the nineteen-eighties, "but I come pretty damn close." ♦

RICHARD OLDDEN, JANUARY 21, 1991

"Just a minute, Phipps! It's <u>my</u> turn to go in and win their confidence."

TOP HARRY BLISS, JANUARY 15, 2007   BOTTOM ALAIN, MARCH 1, 1941

*"I claim this island for the U.S.A. and the
Alfred R. Whipple Real Estate Company of Muscatine, Iowa."*

"Ignore them. They're cartoonists."

TOP I. KLEIN, JULY 11, 1931 BOTTOM TOM KLEH, NOVEMBER 13, 2000

"We couldn't find a raw-vegan, gluten-free, sugar-free, non-G.M.O. cake for your birthday, so we got you nothing."

"It started out with lactose, but now he's intolerant of <u>everything</u>."

TOP P.C. VEY, APRIL 27, 2015   BOTTOM SIDNEY HARRIS, APRIL 14, 1997

"Let's just go in and see what happens."

"Now they're saying shiny things attached to hooks are bad for you."

TOP GEORGE BOOTH, JANUARY 20, 1986   BOTTOM BRUCE KAPLAN, SEPTEMBER 18, 2000

"I'm so hungry I could eat half a sandwich."

PAT BYRNES, SEPTEMBER 21, 1998

"*Lookin' good, Frosty!*"

"*I started my vegetarianism for health reasons,
then it became a moral choice,
and now it's just to annoy people.*"

"*Eat lots of carrots.*"

TOP DANNY SHANAHAN, DECEMBER 27, 1993   MIDDLE ALEX GREGORY, MAY 5, 2003   BOTTOM CHARLES BARSOTTI, JANUARY 29, 1996

"*Then one day he said, 'It's either me or the damned cat!'*"

"*I'm staying together for the sake of my parents.*"

TOP MICK STEVENS, JUNE 22, 1992 BOTTOM LIZA DONNELLY, JULY 25, 2005

"This next song is about love—that special kind of love between a man, his ex-wife, their delinquent children, her attorney, several stockbrokers, and the Internal Revenue Service."

"I was on hormone replacement for two years before I realized that what I really needed was Steve replacement."

TOP TOM CHENEY, SEPTEMBER 1, 2003 BOTTOM JACK ZIEGLER, APRIL 2, 2001

"Some people say you can't put a price on a wife's twenty-seven years of loyalty and devotion. They're wrong."

"I now declare you divorced, reversing my decision of three years ago pronouncing you man and wife."

"My mom has a new boyfriend, my dad has a new girlfriend, and all I got was a new therapist."

TOP LEO CULLUM, MARCH 29, 1993 MIDDLE HENRY MARTIN, MARCH 29, 1993 BOTTOM CHRISTOPHER WEYANT, JANUARY 22, 2001

"Sex brought us together, but gender drove us apart."

BARBARA SMALLER, DECEMBER 10, 2001

"You should relax less."

"Are you sure you're not confusing manic-depressive with awake-asleep?"

TOP DANNY SHANAHAN, MAY 30, 2005 BOTTOM WILLIAM HAEFELI, MARCH 5, 2007

"Ah, Mr. Bromley. Nice to put a face on a disease."

"I don't like the look of these. I better send them up to legal."

TOP MIKE TWOHY, JANUARY 5, 1998 BOTTOM CHRISTOPHER WEYANT, AUGUST 13, 2007

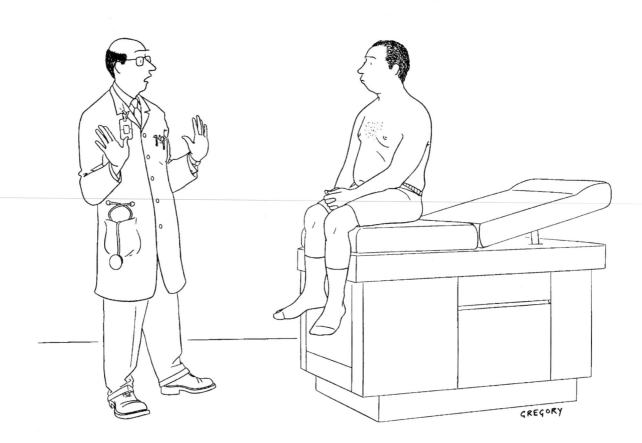

"*Whoa—way too much information.*"

"*My approach is nontraditional, but from a uniquely Western perspective.*"

TOP ALEX GREGORY, APRIL 15, 2002   BOTTOM DAVID SIPRESS, AUGUST 20, 2001

"This stuff worked pretty well on me."

"Although it's nothing serious, let's keep an eye on it
to make sure it doesn't turn into a major lawsuit."

TOP DREW DERNAVICH, MARCH 3, 2003   BOTTOM CHRISTOPHER WEYANT, AUGUST 27, 2007

"Look. They say sit, you sit. They say roll over, you roll over. Where's the prob?"

"Infidel!"

TOP JACK ZIEGLER, APRIL 6, 2009 BOTTOM DANNY SHANAHAN, MAY 2, 2005

"Meow, but don't quote me on that."

"If he has a tell, I haven't found it."

TOP CHRISTOPHER WEYANT, MAY 19, 2003   BOTTOM PAUL NOTH, SEPTEMBER 14, 2015

"*Sheer will, I tell you—sheer will.*"

HARRY BLISS, OCTOBER 27, 2003

"You'll have to phrase it another way.
They have no word for 'fetch.'"

"It'll never work. You're a dog person and I'm a cat person."

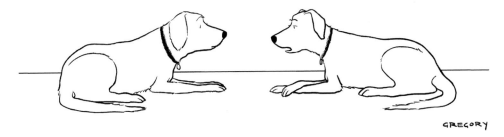

"I would not be opposed to a cat tax."

TOP DREW DERNAVICH, AUGUST 20, 2007   MIDDLE KAAMRAN HAFEEZ, OCTOBER 21, 2013   BOTTOM ALEX GREGORY, MAY 7, 2012

*"Look, I know you and I have had our differences,
but can we at least agree that the goldfish is pointless?"*

"'Grrr' is not a word."

TOP TOM TORO, DECEMBER 1, 2014   BOTTOM SHANNON WHEELER, JULY 2, 2012

D

"Cats have a way of bringing out the dog in me."

TOP MICHAEL MASLIN, JULY 26, 2010   BOTTOM DREW DERNAVICH, APRIL 30, 2012

More Useful Doomsayers

TOP ROZ CHAST, FEBRUARY 17, 2003   BOTTOM KIM WARP, FEBRUARY 11, 2008

TOP MICK STEVENS, OCTOBER 9, 1995 BOTTOM JAMES STEVENSON, JULY 9, 1979

"Oh, my God! Isn't that Dr. Harwood, the famous physicist?"

TOP BOB MANKOFF, OCTOBER 31, 2005   BOTTOM JAMES MULLIGAN, JANUARY 9, 1960

FRANK COTHAM, OCTOBER 20, 1997

"I dreamed that I stopped doing your laundry."

"I thought it was just one of those bad dreams,
but apparently, honey, we have a kid."

TOP VICTORIA ROBERTS, FEBRUARY 4, 2008   BOTTOM JACK ZIEGLER, MAY 11, 1998

"Uh-oh. I think I'm having one of those dreams again."

"On your left."

TOP JACK ZIEGLER, JANUARY 14, 2008   BOTTOM MICHAEL CRAWFORD, NOVEMBER 11, 2002

*The Night Before the Big Meeting Frank
Receives a Visit from the PowerPoint Fairy.*

"I object!"   "Overruled!"

TOP GLEN LE LIEVRE, FEBRUARY 9, 2004 BOTTOM JOSEPH FARRIS, MARCH 16, 1987

*SEE ALSO ASTRONOMY, BEDTIME STORIES, FORTUNE TELLERS

"Last night I dreamed in e-mail."

TOP BOB MANKOFF, NOVEMBER 8, 2004   BOTTOM ROBERT LEIGHTON, DECEMBER 12, 2005

"I said, can I borrow one of your pistols?"

TOP ERIC LEWIS, AUGUST 24, 2009   BOTTOM HARRY BLISS, DECEMBER 10, 2012

"He didn't have to get snippy about it!"

TOP FRANK COTHAM, NOVEMBER 20, 2000   BOTTOM ALAIN, JULY 20, 1940

"Coördinates 135 and 350."

TOP ARNIE LEVIN, JANUARY 21, 200   BOTTOM MISCHA RICHTER, SEPTEMBER 21, 1987

*SEE ALSO COWBOYS, GUNS, JOUSTING

D

"To be on the safe side, let's just say 'noonish.'"

TOP ARNIE LEVIN, SEPTEMBER 29, 1980   BOTTOM BRUCE KAPLAN, FEBRUARY 17, 2003

OTTO SOGLOW, APRIL 28, 1934

EARLY BIRD GETS THE WORM
EASTER BUNNY
EASTER ISLAND
EDGAR ALLAN POE
EDUCATION
EINSTEIN
ELECTIONS
ELEPHANT NEVER FORGETS
ELVIS
ENDANGERED SPECIES
ENVIRONMENT
ETHICS
EUREKA
EVOLUTION
EXECUTIONS
EXPERIMENTS
EYE CHARTS

*"I'm sorry, but you have to be here the minute
the doors open if you want worm."*

*"Yes, I'm still getting up early, but these days it's to check on
the spot markets for oil and natural gas."*

TOP CHARLES BARSOTTI, MARCH 8, 1999   BOTTOM EDWARD KOREN, JUNE 6, 2005

TOP LEO CULLUM, MAY 16, 1994   BOTTOM AL ROSS, APRIL 4, 1994

"My name is Bunny, and I'm a chocoholic."

THE EASTER BUNNY IN AUGUST

TOP DANNY SHANAHAN, APRIL 24, 2000   BOTTOM J.C. DUFFY, AUGUST 23, 2004

"*I like the Easter Bunny—*
I find him less judgmental than Santa Claus."

"*I hear you've been doing exciting things with eggs and dye.*"

TOP BARBARA SMALLER, APRIL 25, 2011 BOTTOM MIKE TWOHY, APRIL 12, 1993

"Easter was last week."

*"Wouldn't you know—the one time I fall in love
with a bunny he turns out to be chocolate."*

TOP GEORGE PRICE, ARPIL 28, 1973   BOTTOM BRUCE KAPLAN, APRIL 8, 1996

"Who hired him?"

"I'm more interested in hearing about the eggs you're hiding from yourself."

TOP JOSEPH FARRIS, DECEMBER 19, 1988   BOTTOM PAUL NOTH, APRIL 13, 2009

"He's in the field today."

"Who you calling a candyass?'"

TOP MIKE TWOHY, APRIL 1, 2002   BOTTOM DANNY SHANAHAN, APRIL 25, 2011

*SEE ALSO BUNNIES, HUMPTY DUMPTY, RAPUNZEL

"I can't imagine why we didn't think of this before."

TOP LEE LORENZ, APRIL 4, 1988 BOTTOM GAHAN WILSON, APRIL 17, 2000

EASTER and PASSOVER ISLAND

"Guess who's getting voted off the island."

TOP ARNIE LEVIN, APRIL 20, 1992   BOTTOM LEE LORENZ, DECEMBER 8, 2008

"Here comes another one."

TOP LEO CULLUM, APRIL 16, 1990 BOTTOM TOM CHENEY, JULY 12, 2004

A STONY GAZE

FEW CARTOONISTS HAVE actually been to Rapa Nui, or Easter Island, yet almost all of them could draw from memory the faces of the looming sculptures on that remote South Pacific isle. Size matters: as with Stonehenge or Machu Picchu, they're on a scale that makes us feel small. But their bold simplicity matters, too. **The figures' chiseled brows and stoic expressions are iconic** and, at the same time, mysterious. How did people come to be on an island thousands of miles away from other land? How did they create their art? And why the long faces? Over the years, cartoonists have tried to sort through the perplexities of Rapa Nui with the best unscientific methods known to man. Robert Kraus laid the foundation in 1967, positing a series of self-portraits by an angular artist. From there, the statues grew, showing off some personality. They'll win any staring contest, but cartoonists won't stop trying to make them crack a smile. ♦

E

CHARLES ADDAMS, JULY 2, 1973

"Wait. I never forget a face—Easter Island, 1722!"

TOP RICHARD McCALLISTER, FEBRUARY 13, 1978   BOTTOM J.C. DUFFY, OCTOBER 11, 2004

CHARLES MARTIN, SEPTEMBER 13, 1969

THE TELL-ALL HEART

Not only did he murder me; he hasn't paid his taxes, he's cheating on his girlfriend, AND he's really mean to his assistant.

SCHWARTZ

"Nevermore. And you can quote me."

TOP BENJAMIN SCHWARTZ, FEBRUARY 1, 2016   BOTTOM ED FISHER, JULY 25, 1988

CHARLES ADDAMS, DECEMBER 12, 1983

"You're going to hate yourself."

EDGAR ALLAN PROZAC

TOP DAVID BORCHART, JUNE 6, 2016   BOTTOM DREW DERNAVICH, NOVEMBER 6, 2006

"One more time."

TOP FARLEY KATZ, JANUARY 25, 2016 BOTTOM CHARLES ADDAMS, MAY 21, 1984

"It may be wrong, but it's how I feel."

"If nothing else, school has prepared me for a lifetime of backpacking."

TOP DAVID SIPRESS, JANUARY 5, 2004 BOTTOM WILLIAM HAEFELI, NOVEMBER 13, 2000

*"So, what are we aiming for, Timmy—
the Nobel Prize or 'Inspected by No. 7'?"*

*"Don't cry, Mom. Lots of parents have children who didn't get into their
first-choice college, and they went on to live happy, fulfilled lives."*

TOP TOM CHENEY, NOVEMBER 25, 2002   BOTTOM BARBARA SMALLER, APRIL 3, 2000

"*Graduates, faculty, parents, creditors...*"

"*I need you to line up by attention span.*"

"*Your daughter is a pain in the ass.*"

TOP ARNIE LEVIN, MAY 24, 1993   MIDDLE WILLIAM HAEFELI, APRIL 3, 2006   BOTTOM HARRY BLISS, DECEMBER 7, 1998

THE BERLITZ GUIDE TO PARENT - TEACHER CONFERENCES

TEACHERESE	ENGLISH
Marches to a different drummer.	Nuts.
Needs to brush up on his people skills.	Homicidal.
Creative.	None too bright.
Very creative.	A moron, actually.
She's a riot!	I can't stand her.
He's doing just fine.	What's your kid's name again?

ROZ CHAST, NOVEMBER 15, 1999

*"We've created a safe, nonjudgmental environment
that will leave you child ill-prepared for real life."*

TOP WILLIAM HAEFELI, DECEMBER 6, 2004   BOTTOM BARBARA SMALLER, DECEMBER 21, 1998

"*An excellent defense. Let's give her the doctorate.*"

"*English lit—how about you?*"

TOP J.B. HANDELSMAN, SEPTEMBER 14, 1987   BOTTOM MIKE TWOHY, SEPTEMBER 14, 1992

Einstein Discovers That Time Can Stop Completely

EINSTEIN AT THE BANK

TOP KIM WARP, APRIL 20, 2009   BOTTOM LEE LORENZ, MARCH 17, 1986

SCIENCE AND SOCIETY ~ 1923

SCHRÖDINGER. PAULI. HEISENBERG PLANCK.

EINSTEIN PONDERS THE MYSTERIES OF SPACE AND TIME

TOP SIDNEY HARRIS, NOVEMBER 28, 1983 BOTTOM ROBERT LEIGHTON, OCTOBER 11, 2010

"You're not _the_ Albert Einstein!"

"You know, Einstein never watched
any great television until after he was forty."

TOP RICHARD TAYLOR, MAY 24, 1952   BOTTOM BRUCE KAPLAN, MAY 10, 1999

"Can you stop that crap? The bison are on the move."

"To *you* it was fast."

TOP P.C. VEY, MAY 30, 2016 BOTTOM ERIC LEWIS, NOVEMBER 13, 2000

"Am I a white man in a red state voting for a black president,
or a blue man in a white state voting for a green president?"

"I'd vote for her, but Election Day is the opening of moose season."

TOP DREW DERNAVICH, OCTOBER 27, 2008   BOTTOM LEO CULLUM, NOVEMBER 3, 2008

"If I'd known he was going to win, I never would have voted for him."

TOP BERNARD SCHOENBAUM, NOVEMBER 13, 2000   BOTTOM BOB MANKOFF, OCTOBER 26, 1992

"At last! After all the debates and polls, it's back to real politics!"

ED FISHER, JANUARY 6, 1997

WILSON

THE APPEARANCE OF INTEGRITY

"If you are a Democrat,
Mrs. Hooper-Smith does the Macarena
during your pancakes."

It's nothing like that, Annie.
I just want to start seeing women from
other swing states for a while."

TOP PETER STEINER, JUNE 5, 2000 MIDDLE GEORGE BOOTH, OCTOBER 21, 1996 BOTTOM MICHAEL CRAWFORD, OCTOBER 21, 1996

"God has chosen to ignore my prayers concerning the outcome of this year's election, and so I feel that I am once again free to be a very bad little boy."

"You have, it would appear, _high_ recognition!"

TOP JACK ZIEGLER, NOVEMBER 30, 1992   BOTTOM DANA FRADON, OCTOBER 20, 1986

*SEE ALSO GOVERNMENT, POLITICIANS, UNCLE SAM

"Please, Senator Fairchild, you have to leave. You lost."

"You don't look as if you voted."

TOP CHARLES SAUERS, JANUARY 10, 1983   BOTTOM VICTORIA ROBERTS, NOVEMBER 9, 1998

"As I get older, I find I rely more and more on these sticky notes to remind me."

"You know the type.
Remembers only what he wants to remember."

TOP ARNIE LEVIN, MARCH 11, 1996   BOTTOM FRANK MODELL, AUGUST 12, 1974

"*Honus Wagner had a lifetime batting average of .329 and wrote 'Lohengrin.' Ask me another.*"

TOP J.B. HANDELSMAN, MAY 23, 1988 BOTTOM J.B. HANDELSMAN, JUNE 14, 1976

"*Once you learn, though, you'll never forget.*"

"*With you everything is déjà vu.*"

"*You remembered!*"

TOP CHARLIE HANKIN, AUGUST 10, 2015   MIDDLE FRANK MODELL, OCTOBER 8, 1979   BOTTOM FRANK MODELL, JANUARY 9, 1965

"There's a character in this town I'd like to catch up with—
a snub-nosed, freckle-faced, barefooted little upstart in blue denims,
goddam handy with a slingshot. I guess."

WHITNEY DARROW, JR., JULY 3, 1948

"And this is Brother Elvis."

TOP J.C. DUFFY, JULY 12, 2010　BOTTOM DANNY SHANAHAN, DECEMBER 23, 1991

"I hear we've had another rash of Elvis sightings."

CHICKEN À LA KING

TOP LEE LORENZ, MARCH 27, 1995 BOTTOM DANNY SHANAHAN, JUNE 12, 1989

IRONIC

NON-IRONIC

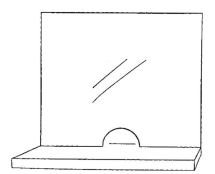

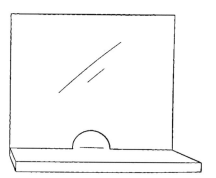

GREGORY

ALEX GREGORY, DECEMBER 25, 2000

"I think the Elvis business
has just about run its course."

"Dearly Besequinned..."

Elvis imitators from that universe
where Elvis was dull, had an M.B.A.,
and couldn't sing.

TOP JAMES STEVENSON, JULY 27, 1992   MIDDLE DANNY SHANAHAN, OCTOBER 30, 1995   BOTTOM DAVID BORCHART, NOVEMBER 30, 2009

*"Pay no attention to what they say.
Spotted owls aren't any better than you are."*

"We have to believe we're not endangered or we'll all go mad."

TOP DONALD REILLY, JUNE 22, 1992   BOTTOM BRUCE KAPLAN, JANUARY 28, 2002

*"It's made from an endangered species for
that one person in a thousand who couldn't care less."*

"My lawyer finally got me on the endangered-species list!"

TOP ROBERT WEBER, DECEMBER 7, 1992 BOTTOM MICK STEVENS, JULY 8, 1996

"That may be, but if you-know-who loses
his protected status we're all out on our butts."

"It's that 'rarer than thou' attitude that gets me."

TOP DANNY SHANAHAN, MARCH 22, 1993   BOTTOM WARREN MILLER, SEPTEMBER 30, 1991

*SEE ALSO BEACHED WHALES, GLOBAL WARMING, ZOOS

"But can they save themselves?"

"Your generous donation," said the Dodo,
"will help us in our quest to find a cure for extinction."

TOP ELDON DEDINI, MAY 23, 1983   BOTTOM J.B. HANDELSMAN, SEPTEMBER 7, 1992

*"Please help us reduce our garbage and improve our
energy efficiency and our water quality.
Help us to be eco-wise and—above all—to empower others."*

"It's a pity those awful people were right about the environment."

TOP EDWARD KOREN, OCTOBER 31, 1994 BOTTOM GAHAN WILSON, OCTOBER 9, 2006

"Nice, but we'll need an environmental-impact study, a warranty, recall bulletins, recycling facilities, and twenty-four-hour customer support."

"Can't we just dye the smoke green?"

TOP TOM CHENEY, APRIL 5, 2007   BOTTOM ROB ESMAY, MAY 14, 2007

"*I try to do my part.*"

"*So this is the famous environment everyone's so hyped up about?*"

"*O.K., now I need a few shots of you looking concerned about the planet.*"

TOP JASON PATTERSON, AUGUST 27, 2007   MIDDLE DAVID SIPRESS, SEPTEMBER 11, 2000   BOTTOM MICHAEL CRAWFORD, AUGUST 2, 1993

"So that's where it goes! Well, I'd like to thank you
fellows for bringing this to my attention."

JAMES STEVENSON, NOVEMBER 7, 1970

"Something's just not right—our air is clean, our water is pure,
we all get plenty of exercise, everything we eat
is organic and free-range, and yet nobody lives past thirty."

"This would be a great place to put a huge city."

TOP ALEX GREGORY, MAY 22, 2006   BOTTOM MATTHEW DIFFEE, MAY 14, 2007

"Oh God, here they come—act green."

"I hated how they acted so much 'greener than thou.'"

TOP BRUCE KAPLAN, AUGUST 20, 2007   BOTTOM WILLIAM HAMILTON, FEBRUARY 11, 2008

"But how do you know for sure you've got power unless you abuse it?"

"Oh, what the hell, I'll add another zero."

TOP BOB MANKOFF, NOVEMBER 16, 1992   BOTTOM P.C. VEY, APRIL 3, 2006

"*Remember, we can only afford to do all this pro bono because of how much anti bono pays.*"

"*Try as we might, sir, our team of management consultants has been unable to find a single fault in the manner in which you conduct your business.*"

TOP PAT BYRNES, JANUARY 3, 2005 BOTTOM J.B. HANDELSMAN, SEPTEMBER 12, 1970

"Here it is—the plain, unvarnished truth. Varnish it."

RICHARD CLINE, JUNE 21, 1999

"Miss Dugan, will you send someone in here
who can distinguish right from wrong?"

"'Honesty is the best policy.' O.K.!
Now, what's the <u>second</u>-best policy?"

TOP DANA FRADON, MARCH 24, 1975 BOTTOM DANA FRADON, MAY 15, 1978

"Eureka! The E.P.A. willing."

"Eureka! Pass it on!"

TOP DANA FRADON, OCTOBER 9, 1978   BOTTOM ED FISHER, APRIL 4, 1970

*SEE ALSO MUSES, SCIENTISTS IN LAB, THINKING OUTSIDE THE BOX

"Eureka! Another sticky, gooey mess!"

"A possible eureka."

TOP DEAN VIETOR, SEPTEMBER 3, 1979   BOTTOM JAMES STEVENSON, AUGUST 22, 1988

"Gee, evolution is slow."

TOP MORT GERBERG, AUGUST 24, 1992   BOTTOM BOB MANKOFF, AUGUST 11, 1980

"Trust me—you're more than ready."

TOP DANNY SHANAHAN, JULY 23, 2001

ONWARD AND UPWARD

T HE ANCESTOR OF the Evolution Gag, Rudolph Zallinger's "March of Progress"—an iconic 1965 foldout from Time-Life's "Early Man" volume—is a nifty little parade that includes an ape at the far left, a Neanderthal near the center, and the Man in the Gray Flannel Suit leading the pack into the future. **A single image with a sequential narrative that even a Cro-Magnon could follow.** It stuck.

It stuck because it promoted the conceited conceit that we are the chosen species journeying forever upward—which is clearly a misplaced hypothesis, judging from the number of people witnessed clipping their toenails on the F train. As a meme, it was later employed by advertisers (Guinness), movie studios ("Encino Man"), rock bands (the Doors' "Full Circle"), and, naturally, cartoonists, who again and again modified the image to bring Man back down where he belongs—in the primordial ooze.

As Peter Steiner's cartoon underlines, we may have risen from depths lower than the subway, but we've only made it to Midtown on a workday. And, although we have shed our fins and gills, we continue to leave behind telltale toenail clippings. Shakespeare anticipated the sober truth of evolution: "From hour to hour, we ripe and ripe, And then, from hour to hour, we rot and rot; And thereby hangs a tale." Or, in this case, a gag. ◆

PETER STEINER, JULY 30, 1990

"*I still say it's only a theory.*"

TOP SAM GROSS, JUNE 17, 2002 BOTTOM DAVID SIPRESS, MAY 23, 2005

"Elitist!"

"Because I've already said all I can say in this particular medium."

TOP WARD SUTTON, SEPTEMBER 8, 2008 MIDDLE MORT GERBERG, MARCH 20, 1995 BOTTOM ED FISHER, DECEMBER 31, 1955

"Say when."

TOP FRANK COTHAM, DECEMBER 7, 1998   BOTTOM TOM CHENEY, AUGUST 26, 1996

"Not now!"

"Last tweet?"

TOP MISCHA RICHTER, FEBRUARY 5, 1966 BOTTOM DAVID SIPRESS, JUNE 1, 2009

"There's no shooting—we just make you keep smoking."

"It's publish or perish, and he hasn't published."

TOP MICHAEL SHAW, NOVEMBER 12, 2001   BOTTOM MISCHA RICHTER, MAY 28, 1966

"Although I leave my current position reluctantly, I have no regrets, and look forward to the exciting new challenges ahead."

"I brought my own bag."

TOP LEE LORENZ, DECEMBER 24, 2007 BOTTOM MICHAEL SHAW, NOVEMBER 8, 2010

"The drug has, however,
proved more effective than traditional psychoanalysis."

PAUL
NOTH

"I don't usually volunteer for experiments,
but I'm kind of a puzzle freak."

TOP PAUL NOTH, JUNE 2, 2008   BOTTOM MIKE TWOHY, SEPTEMBER 23, 2002

"Of course it's much too early to draw conclusions.
The Harvard entrance examinations will tell the story."

"Dr. Steinhauser's experiments are concerned with the
possibility of converting toxic chemical waste into booze."

TOP ROBERT DAY, SEPTEMBER 22, 1934   BOTTOM JOSEPH MIRACHI, AUGUST 20, 1990

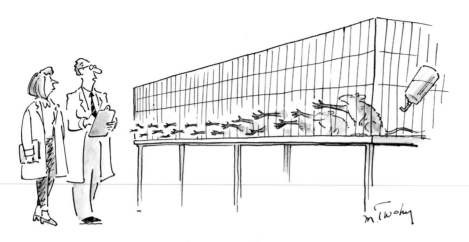

"At this point, we know it's addictive."

"Don't be impatient, sir. Eventually one of them is bound to come up with something."

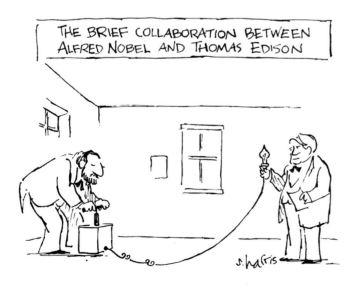

THE BRIEF COLLABORATION BETWEEN ALFRED NOBEL AND THOMAS EDISON

TOP MIKE TWOHY, JANUARY 21, 2008   MIDDLE BRUCE PETTY, SEPTEMBER 23, 1961   BOTTOM SIDNEY HARRIS, NOVEMBER 7, 1988

"Well, Carpenter, this does it!
You and O'Callaghan are through as a team!"

HENRY MARTIN, APRIL 25, 1977

TOP SAUL STEINBERG, SEPTEMBER 29, 2003   BOTTOM ARNIE LEVIN, DECEMBER 24, 1979

TOP LEO CULLUM, AUGUST 8, 1988 BOTTOM OTTO SOGLOW, NOVEMBER 8, 1947

"*Certainly I can make it out!*
It's three sea horses and an 'h.'"

TOP JAMES STEVENSON, NOVEMBER 22, 1958   BOTTOM JAMES THURBER, MARCH 6, 1937

"By George, it is 'n'! It always looked like an 'm' to me."

TOP CHON DAY, FEBRUARY 24, 1945 BOTTOM JACK ZIEGLER, NOVEMBER 29, 2004

FACEBOOK
FAMILY
FAMOUS PAINTERS & PAINTINGS
FASHION
FEMINISM
FINANCE
FITNESS
FOOD
FOOTBALL
FORTUNE TELLER
FOUNTAIN OF YOUTH
FRANKENSTEIN
FREUD
FUNERALS

"His Highness is changing his relationship status."

"Why can't you use Facebook, like everybody else?"

TOP DAVID SIPRESS, DECEMBER 20, 2010   BOTTOM WARD SUTTON, MAY 11, 2009

"I'm too busy recommending things to experience them myself."

"I promise to love, honor, and stay the hell off Facebook."

TOP ROBERT LEIGHTON, AUGUST 1, 2011   BOTTOM DARRIN BELL, MARCH 7, 2016

"I lost all my Facebook friends after I asked them to lend me some money."

"Just sitting here waiting for Facebook to go away."

TOP BOB MANKOFF, FEBRUARY 25, 2008   BOTTOM BRUCE KAPLAN, JUNE 8, 2009

"Now go to the comment box under your picture and type,
'No matter what you've been hearing, I'm really a very nice person.'"

"Yes, you've mentioned this 'Facebook' in the past—
tell me, is 'Facebook' saying anything right now?"

TOP DAVID SIPRESS, APRIL 18, 2011   BOTTOM SARA LAUTMAN, OCTOBER 3, 2016

*"Your mother and I are feeling overwhelmed,
so you'll have to bring yourselves up."*

"Oh, Christ—it's your mother."

TOP DAVID SIPRESS, FEBRUARY 8, 1999 BOTTOM HARRY BLISS, NOVEMBER 29, 2004

"If you can hear me, give me a sign."

*"I've spent so much time with family that I've started
to lose sight of what really matters."*

TOP FRANK COTHAM, DECEMBER 13, 1993   BOTTOM MATTHEW DIFFEE, JANUARY 24, 2005

"You're why I have the moat, Mother."

"Hi, Dad. Investment banking wasn't
that great after all."

"They got extinct because they didn't
listen to their mommies."

TOP CHARLES BARSOTTI, JUNE 26, 2006   MIDDLE PETER STEINER, FEBRUARY 29, 1988   BOTTOM DONALD REILLY, JANUARY 27, 2003

"Young man, go to your room and
stay there until your cerebral cortex matures."

"I'm their real child, and you're just a frozen embryo thingy
they bought from some laboratory."

TOP BARBARA SMALLER, APRIL 24, 2006   BOTTOM WILLIAM HAMILTON, JANUARY 19, 1998

"*Thank you, Adrian. Parenting is a learning process, and your criticisms help.*"

"*Am I the smart one and you're the pretty one or is it the other way around?*"

TOP ROBERT WEBER, AUGUST 10, 1998   BOTTOM BARBARA SMALLER, JANUARY 24, 2000

*SEE ALSO PSYCHIATRISTS, QUARRELS

"No, I don't want to know what my approval rating is."

PORTUGUESE MOM OF WAR

TOP DANA FRADON, SEPTEMBER 25, 2000   BOTTOM DANNY SHANAHAN, JULY 24, 2006

"David looks positively Manet-ish in that boater. Or is it Monet-ish?"

"Now, there's a nice contemporary sunset!"

TOP MORT GERBERG, AUGUST 2, 1976   BOTTOM JAMES STEVENSON, AUGUST 29, 1964

"He does have a point."

THE CRITICS SPOTTED THE BOGUS
ROTHKO ALMOST IMMEDIATELY.

TOP MICHAEL CRAWFORD, SEPTEMBER 28, 2009   BOTTOM GLEN BAXTER, AUGUST 18, 2003

FRAMED

J OKES ABOUT FAMOUS WORKS OF ART allow the cartoonist to settle an old score—the perennial, tiresome question of whether or not cartoons are *art*. Funny things just don't give you the feeling you're supposed to have when looking at capital-A Art; you're supposed to feel awe, to feel dwarfed. Comedy, on the other hand, brings you in; it sympathizes with you, cultivates a warmth toward your fellow man—those of them clever enough to laugh along, anyway. It's fun, the prevailing wisdom goes, but it ain't classy. Shut out of the rarefied air of the salon, cartoonists get to work doing what they do best: taking the bastards down a peg. This isn't done without affection; most cartoonists, after all, got into the game in part because they love drawing and painting. Gags about iconic pieces of art let the air out of the snob's tires while establishing the cartoonist's own artsy-fartsy bona fides. **If you can't beat them, draw them.** ♦

"*Van Gogh was a good painter, but he couldn't draw trains.*"

WARREN MILLER, NOVEMBER 12, 1984

"You will find more on the floor above."

"Oh, it's you."

TOP ROBERT DAY, MARCH 4, 1967   BOTTOM SAM GROSS, MAY 2, 1994

"Then what happened?"

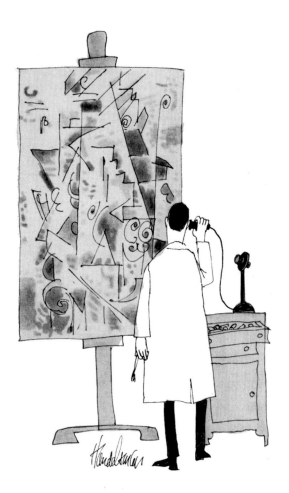

"Hello, Braque? Picasso here. Cubism is out."

TOP BARNEY TOBEY, MAY 9, 1964 BOTTOM J.B. HANDELSMAN, OCTOBER 25, 1969

"Does this dress make me look Republican?"

"I can't walk in these shoes, which is a problem,
because I can't sit down in this skirt."

TOP MATTHEW DIFFEE, OCTOBER 18, 2004   BOTTOM BARBARA SMALLER, SEPTEMBER 22, 2003

"I paid three grand for this dress—I'll wear it wherever I want!"

"I'm on Fendi and Prada, and heading toward Louis."

TOP CAROLITA JOHNSON, MAY 8, 2006   BOTTOM MARISA ACOCELLA, MARCH 18, 2002

THE LOVE SONG OF
J. ALFRED CREW

ROZ CHAST, APRIL 24, 1995

"I say one or the other. But leopardskin and heels is too much."

"Loved Jamaica!"

"It's all marketing—no one actually wears that stuff."

TOP PETER STEINER, MARCH 30, 1998   MIDDLE FELIPE GALINDO, SEPTEMBER 29, 2003   BOTTOM LEO CULLUM, MARCH 20, 2006

"I love you, too, Daddy, but it just kills me that you're a man."

"Books by men are in the basement."

TOP DANNY SHANAHAN, FEBRUARY 26, 1996   BOTTOM DONALD REILLY, MAY 17, 1993

"*I can't cook, but I can pay.*"

"*Yes, I realize that we are free agents, but I have to take on the additional risk of pregnancy and am more susceptible to certain sexually transmitted diseases, so I think you should pay for the movie.*"

TOP BRUCE KAPLAN, MAY 10, 1993 BOTTOM BARBARA SMALLER, NOVEMBER 20, 2000

"My wife works, and I sit on the eggs. Want to make something of it?"

"It seems to me that ordination of women might brighten the place up a bit."

TOP CHON DAY, AUGUST 2, 1993   BOTTOM ED FISHER, JANUARY 17, 2000

"Aha! Just as I suspected!"

"All I really want is control over my own body!"

TOP BOB MANKOFF, MAY 22, 1995   BOTTOM EDWARD KOREN, DECEMBER 10, 2001

"Well, I was outvoted by the stockholders today by eight thousand six hundred and twenty-seven to one."

"And this is where we adjust the interest rate."

TOP JACK ZIEGLER, DECEMBER 1, 1986   BOTTOM JASON PATTERSON, OCTOBER 25, 2010

THE SWISS BANKERS' CONVENTION

"Something's happened, Doug. I've lost touch with the Warren Buffett in me."

TOP JAMES STEVENSON, JUNE 16, 2003   BOTTOM ROBERT WEBER, OCTOBER 9, 1995

"*Personally, I liked this roller coaster a lot better before the Federal Reserve Board got hold of it.*"

"*I'm getting subtle hints of what the Fed might do.*"

TOP BOB MANKOFF, JUNE 9, 1997   BOTTOM PAUL NOTH, APRIL 20, 2015

*SEE ALSO BANKS, LOTTERIES, MOBSTERS

AT HOME WITH
BEN BERNANKE

*"And if you think that every time you open your mouth
around here everyone is going to dance to your tune,
you've got another thing coming, Mr. Federal Reserve!"*

F

*"Do you swear to calm the jittery financial markets, all the jittery financial markets
and nothing but the jittery financial markets, so help you God?"*

TOP DAVID SIPRESS, OCTOBER 7, 2013   BOTTOM MICHAEL CRAWFORD, FEBRUARY 4, 2008

JASON.

"I usually do two hours of cardio and then four more
of cardio and then two more of cardio."

"I don't speak Yoga. I speak Pilates."

TOP JASON POLAN, MARCH 6, 2006   BOTTOM DAVID SIPRESS, SEPTEMBER 22, 2003

"I was able to get in one last lecture about diet and exercise."

TOP FRANK COTHAM, MAY 29, 2006   BOTTOM MORT GERBERG, JULY 20, 1998

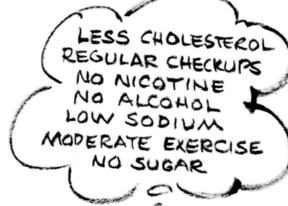

LEE LORENZ, FEBRUARY 20, 1989

"Be honest—how much are you exercising?"

"I'm thinking of doing Pamplona this year."

TOP CHARLES BARSOTTI, MARCH 27, 2006   BOTTOM ARNIE LEVIN, JULY 5, 1999

"*Fusilli, you crazy bastard! How are you?*"

"*Hey, everybody, we're invited to a cookout!*"

TOP CHARLES BARSOTTI, NOVEMBER 21, 1994   BOTTOM CHARLES BARSOTTI, JULY 20, 1998

398

"It's your ribs. I'm afraid they're delicious."

"It's broccoli, dear."
"I say it's spinach, and I say the hell with it."

TOP PAUL NOTH, NOVEMBER 23, 2009 BOTTOM CARL ROSE, DECEMBER 8, 1928

"This is mastodon. I told you to get mammoth."

"And that's how you make a peanut-butter sandwich."

TOP ALEX GREGORY, SEPTEMBER 3, 2007   BOTTOM TOM CHENEY, NOVEMBER 23, 2009

*SEE ALSO ICE CREAM, KETCHUP, ORANGES VS. APPLES

"We would like to be genetically modified to taste like Brussels sprouts."

TOP SAM GROSS, MARCH 6, 2000   BOTTOM SIDNEY HARRIS, FEBRUARY 8, 1999

*"It's a game of power, speed, agility, and grace,
but, most of all, Tom, it's a game of points."*

*"I'm glad we won, and I hope that someday we'll have a
university that our football team can be proud of."*

TOP JACK ZIEGLER, JANUARY 5, 1998   BOTTOM BORIS DRUCKER, NOVEMBER 10, 1997

"Football takes my mind off baseball."

"My client wants a fifty-per-cent salary boost, a bonus guarantee,
and a snappy choreographed victory dance he can do after he makes a touchdown."

TOP DAVID SIPRESS, OCTOBER 28, 2002   BOTTOM JAMES STEVENSON, SEPTEMBER 24, 1990

"But what if that guy in the bleachers is right? What if I do suck?"

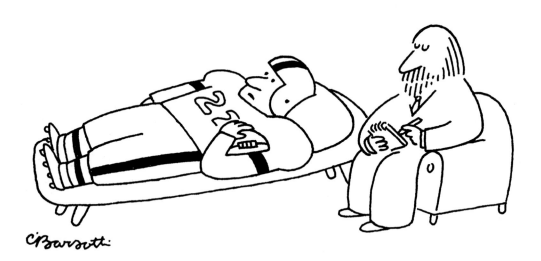

*"Then I wake up, the cheering has stopped,
I have three kids, and I work in a cubicle."*

"Hey, kids! Grandpa's on TV."

TOP EDWARD FRASCINO, AUGUST 21, 2000   BOTTOM CHARLES BARSOTTI, NOVEMBER 18, 1991

"You will be going on a long walk."

*"You will make the same foolish mistakes you have made before,
not only once but many, many times again."*

TOP ARNIE LEVIN, MAY 27, 1991   BOTTOM GAHAN WILSON, JANUARY 18, 2010

"Nothing will ever happen to you."

"How frustrating. The crystal ball is down again."

TOP WHITNEY DARROW, JR., DECEMBER 26, 1977   BOTTOM ROBERT WEBER, AUGUST 12, 1991

WHAT NEXT?

OUR CAVE ANCESTORS searched the skies for omens; modern man turns, pleading, to Nate Silver. The desire to know the future is as much a part of humanity as the desires for sex and food. In fact, it speaks to those desires: in the future, will I have enough sex and food? Attempts to predict the future are, at bottom, attempts to control it: What can I do to ensure that I have more sex and food, or at least to prevent sex and food from being taken away from me?

The storefront psychic promises relief from uncertainty. **We know she's a sham, but a little part of us hopes that maybe, just maybe, she's got the goods.** Cartoons depicting the psychic and her customer allow us to laugh knowingly at the dupe in the mark's chair, but they also allow us to laugh a little at ourselves—at that ancient part of us that still believes a shaman can help us figure out our sex-food situation. It's a harmless bit of fun that allows us to acknowledge the raw fear of what's to come. And, besides, fortune tellers are more fun to draw than statisticians. ♦

"Sorry—that's the screen saver."

DREW DERNAVICH, MAY 28, 2007

"Sometimes the future is bright, sometimes it's dark—it's all cyclical."

*"According to an article in the upcoming issue of
The New England Journal of Medicine, all your fears are well founded."*

TOP FRANK COTHAM, MARCH 26, 2001   BOTTOM MICHAEL MASLIN, JUNE 7, 1993

*SEE ALSO MAGICIANS, QUESTIONS, WITCHES' CAULDRON

F

"You will never catch up with the new technology."

ROBERT WEBER, FEBRUARY 14, 1983

411

"Wifey! Wifey! I've found the fountain of youth!"

TOP ROZ CHAST, APRIL 8, 1991   BOTTOM WARREN MILLER, FEBRUARY 9, 1976

"So we've discovered the Fountain of Youth. Who's going to sail the old tub back?"

CHARLES ADDAMS, MARCH 21, 1977

"It's better than nothing, I guess."

"Can it be that we've discovered the fountain of youth, General?"

TOP DANA FRADON, JANUARY 16, 1971   BOTTOM MISCHA RICHTER, SEPTEMBER 11, 1943

TOP ROZ CHAST, APRIL 18, 2016   BOTTOM MATTHEW DIFFEE, NOVEMBER 8, 2010

"Bring me a stem cell."

"You're incredibly tight."

TOP JASON PATTERSON, MAY 14, 2007   BOTTOM DANNY SHANAHAN, DECEMBER 17, 2001

"Well, we got the grant."

TOP DAVID SIPRESS, FEBRUARY 7, 2011   BOTTOM ARNIE LEVIN, JANUARY 30, 1989

"Some Debussy, Igor."

"He goes to the bathroom a lot. Where did you get the kidneys?"

TOP GEORGE BOOTH, MARCH 17, 1997   BOTTOM SAM GROSS, NOVEMBER 26, 2007

"It's the co-op board!"

"Remember how big and clunky the first ones were?"

TOP NICK DOWNES, JULY 26, 1999   BOTTOM DANNY SHANAHAN, SEPTEMBER 13, 1999

*"Don't you think, Doctor, in view of my marked improvement
I might resume my affection for my mother?"*

*"Oh, he's, like, primarily a Freudian, I guess you could say,
but he vibrates to the other disciplines as well."*

TOP ALAN DUNN, FEBRUARY 23, 1929 BOTTOM EVERETT OPIE, OCTOBER 9, 1971

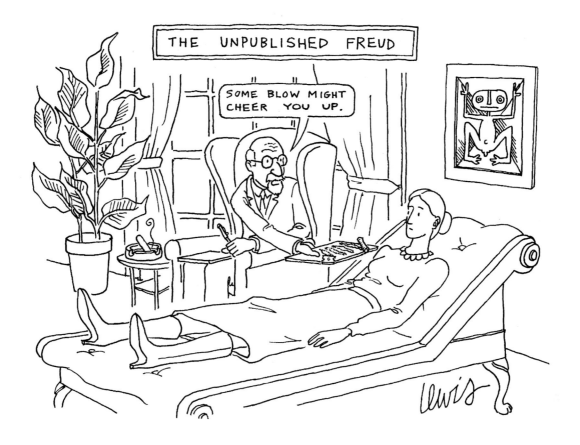

"Well, 'Dr. Freud' is off and running again!"

TOP ERIC LEWIS, MARCH 11, 2002   BOTTOM JAMES MULLIGAN, JULY 14, 1962

*"Now, remember, Ed, you symbolize the superego, and you,
Tom, represent the evil forces lurking in the id."*

WHITNEY DARROW, JR., APRIL 2, 1960

"Light on the id, heavy on the super-ego."

"I will, however, say this for Freud—he got a lot of people thinking."

TOP KENNETH MAHOOD, JANUARY 7, 1974   BOTTOM DONALD REILLY, OCTOBER 24, 1983

REQUIEM FOR A LIGHTWEIGHT

TOP FRANK COTHAM, MAY 8, 1995   BOTTOM MICHAEL CRAWFORD, AUGUST 24, 1992

*"It's an unusual request, but, yes, for an additional consideration
I'm sure we can have him arranged on a bed of arugula."*

"He brought joy to tens."

TOP DONALD REILLY, JANUARY 8, 1990   BOTTOM BRUCE KAPLAN, JANUAR 5, 2015

"We are gathered here today to bid farewell to the best assistant any magician could ask for."

"It looks nothing like him."

TOP TOM CHENEY, MAY 10, 2010   BOTTOM DANNY SHANAHAN, DECEMBER 2, 2002

"But, seriously…"

TOP JACK ZIEGLER, JULY 11, 1994   BOTTOM JOHN JONIK, MAY 13, 1996

GEORGE PRICE, NOVEMBER 19, 1949

GALLEY SLAVES
GAY MARRIAGE
GENERALS
GLOBAL WARMING
GODZILLA
GOLDFISH BOWLS
GOLDILOCKS
GOLF
GOOD COP, BAD COP
GOOGLE
GOVERNMENT
G.P.S.
GRADUATION
GRAMMAR
GREEK MYTHOLOGY
GRIM REAPER
GROUNDHOG DAY
GUNS

"Grueling as this is, it's not a total-body workout."

"It's definitely a change of tactics, but the overall strategy remains the same."

TOP ALEX GREGORY, JULY 3, 2000   BOTTOM LEE LORENZ, NOVEMBER 13, 2006

"Excellent. Now just the altos."

"Listen, pal. That 'all in the same boat' crack
wasn't funny even the first time."

TOP CHRISTOPHER WEYANT, MAY 14, 2001   BOTTOM SMILBY, MARCH 17, 1962

"7-D? Yes, you're right here, on the outside."

"We get it, Tom—you're management now."

TOP WARREN MILLER, MARCH 15, 1969   BOTTOM DAVID BORCHART, APRIL 7, 2008

"I don't know how you feel, but I hate these company outings."

WARREN MILLER, SEPTEMBER 18, 1965

"You knew I was straight when you married me."

"Do you have any California wines that support same-sex marriage?"

TOP DAVID SIPRESS, AUGUST 9, 2004   BOTTOM CHRISTOPHER WEYANT, JUNE 29, 2009

"I wouldn't marry you if you were the last gay person on earth!"

*"There's nothing wrong with our marriage, but the spectre of gay marriage
has hopelessly eroded the institution."*

TOP AL ROSS, JULY 15, 1996   BOTTOM BOB MANKOFF, JULY 26, 2004

WILLIAM HAEFELI, NOVEMBER 17, 2003

"Look, I'd like to avoid overkill, but not at the risk of underkill."

TOP BOB MANKOFF, DECEMBER 3, 2001 BOTTOM JOSEPH FARRIS, MAY 31, 1999

"Let's run it up the flagpole and see if anyone shoots at it."

"The answer isn't more troops—what you need is an antibiotic."

TOP CHRISTOPHER WEYANT, JULY 26, 2004   BOTTOM FRANK COTHAM, DECEMBER 14, 2009

"A four-star general must be a very good general indeed."

PETER STEINER, DECEMBER 21, 1998

*SEE ALSO MILITARY MEDALS

"I just got a great idea for a war!"

"I, on the other hand, find it frustrating that we have
more missiles than we know what to do with."

TOP MICK STEVENS, JULY 7, 2003   BOTTOM AL ROSS, JANUARY 16, 1984

TELLTALE SIGNS OF GLOBAL WARMING

GREGORY

MANKOFF

"Long term I'm worried about global warming—short term, about freezing my ass off."

TOP ALEX GREGORY, MARCH 7, 2005   BOTTOM BOB MANKOFF, FEBRUARY 19, 2007

"I'm starting to get concerned about global warming."

TOP LEE LORENZ, DECEMBER 25, 2006   BOTTOM SAM GROSS, JUNE 1, 1998

"Call this an iceberg? When I was a kid we
wouldn't have called this an iceberg!"

"Gentlemen, it's time we gave some serious thought to the effects of global warming."

*SEE ALSO ENVIRONMENT, HEAT WAVES, POLLUTION

"In the next five years, global warming is going to make you ten times more irritating."

Rising Sea Levels — An Alternative Theory

TOP BRUCE KAPLAN, JULY 10, 2006   BOTTOM KIM WARP, AUGUST 28, 2006

"*I wish I had that kind of energy.*"

"*O.K., O.K., let's take the F.D.R.*"

TOP P.C. VEY, AUGUST 15, 2011 BOTTOM JASON PATTERSON, APRIL 21, 2008

"I'm not sure if the audience is ready to embrace you in a romantic comedy."

"Let's face it—the city's in our blood."

TOP ALEX GREGORY, APRIL 28, 2008   BOTTOM DANNY SHANAHAN, DECEMBER 15, 1997

"Lou, c'mere—you gotta check out this guy's Degas!"

TOP JASON PATTERSON, MARCH 16, 2009 BOTTOM HARRY BLISS, JULY 3, 2006

"I hear he's huge in Japan."

TOP DANNY SHANAHAN, FEBRUARY 9, 2004   BOTTOM PAUL NOTH, DECEMBER 25, 2006

"Let's go around one more time and then call it a day."

TOP SAM GROSS, MAY 26, 1973   BOTTOM JOHN NORMENT, AUGUST 23, 1976

*"She's not his wife. She ate his wife the first day
we put her in with them."*

TOP MIKE TWOHY, NOVEMBER 21, 1983   BOTTOM HELEN HOKINSON, SEPTEMBER 18, 1937

"Kim! Small world!"

TOP ARNIE LEVIN, SEPTEMBER 5, 1983   BOTTOM JASON ADAM KATZENSTEIN, APRIL 20, 2015

MICHAEL CRAWFORD, JUNE 2, 2003

*"They're offering a deal—you pay court costs and damages,
they drop charges of breaking and entering."*

*"We are in the bears' house. Goldilocks has just eaten
a bowl of porridge. Papa Bear enters."*

TOP MICHAEL MASLIN, FEBRUARY 1, 1988   BOTTOM MICK STEVENS, DECEMBER 24, 2001

TOP CHARLES ADDAMS, JANUARY 8, 1979   BOTTOM DANNY SHANAHAN, JULY 12, 2010

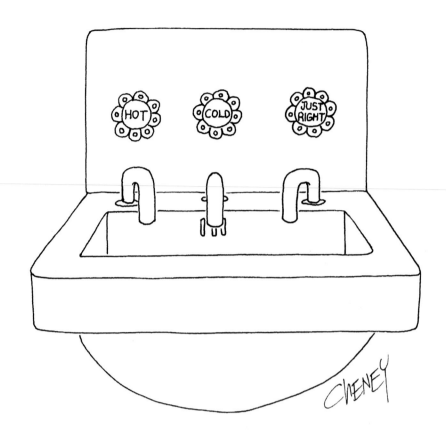

"Someone's been sleeping in my bed, too, and there she is on Screen Nine!"

TOP TOM CHENEY, MARCH 28, 1983   BOTTOM DANNY SHANAHAN, FEBRUARY 13, 1989

*SEE ALSO CINDERELLA, HUMPTY DUMPTY, WISHING WELL

I remember well my sensation as we first entered the house. I knew instantly that something was very wrong. I realized that my father's chair had been sat in, as well as my mother's and my own. The porridge we had left on the table to cool had been partially eaten. None of this, however, prepared me for what we were about to discover upstairs. . . .

WHITNEY DARROW, JR., AUGUST 6, 1979

"Go with two-iron, Kemosabe—distance in desert not what it seems."

*"Researchers say I'm not happier for being richer,
but do you know how much researchers make?"*

"Here's one you'll understand."

*"Gotta run, sweetheart. By the way, that was one
fabulous job you did raising the children."*

TOP CLAUDE SMITH, NOVEMBER 22, 1958   BOTTOM ROBERT WEBER, MAY 4, 1992

*"I've decided to return to my first passion in life—
selling drugs to kids."*

"If you're so enlightened, how come you can't lick that slice?"

TOP MATTHEW DIFFEE, APRIL 3, 2000   BOTTOM SAM GROSS, JANUARY 2, 1989

HOLE IN FORTY-SEVEN

RESUME COUNTING

TOP CLAUDE SMITH, MAY 21, 1960   MIDDLE MICK STEVENS, AUGUST 21, 2000   BOTTOM MISCHA RICHTER, AUGUST 13, 1955

"I'm neither a good cop nor a bad cop, Jerome. Like yourself, I'm a complex amalgam of positive and negative personality traits that emerge or not, depending on circumstances."

"No doubt you already know if I'm a good cop or a bad cop."

TOP MICK STEVENS, JULY 30, 2007   BOTTOM CAROLITA JOHNSON, DECEMBER 17, 2012

"Sometimes I can't remember if I'm good cop or bad cop."

"So where's the good cop?"

TOP CHRISTOPHER WEYANT, NOVEMBER 3, 2008   BOTTOM GAHAN WILSON, AUGUST 18, 2003

GOOD STRIPPER COP / BAD STRIPPER COP

GOOD FIREMAN, BAD FIREMAN

TOP ZACHARY KANIN, JUNE 2, 2008   BOTTOM ERIC LEWIS, JULY 2, 2012

GOOD COP, GREAT COP

TOP MICHAEL CRAWFORD, AUGUST 29, 2005   BOTTOM DANNY SHANAHAN, JANUARY 15, 2001

"Would you like to see the top on Google Earth?"

"I'm giving up Google for Lent."

TOP DAVID SIPRESS, OCTOBER 1, 2007   BOTTOM VICTORIA ROBERTS, FEBRUARY 19, 2007

"I can't explain it—it's just a funny feeling that I'm being Googled."

TOP CHARLES BARSOTTI, OCTOBER 28, 2002   BOTTOM ROZ CHAST, NOVEMBER 30, 2009

I'M FEELING LUCKY

THE INTERNET has changed our world more than any other modern invention, and standing astride the digital landscape is our benevolent overlord, Google. **No other company has so thoroughly dominated our lives.** Think of the million things you outsource to its products—the search engine, the mail client, the maps—and wonder how you ever lived without them. Google's ubiquity, its fun-to-say name, and its creepily optimistic corporate culture are all catnip to cartoonists, who, after all, spend a good part of the day Googling their own names.

The company motto, of course, has long been "Don't be evil." That Google feels it must, on a corporate level, remind itself not to be evil gives one pause; one is immediately alerted to the possibility that it is, in fact, evil as hell. Indeed, as a species, we've arrived at the understanding, bordering on axiomatic, that technology will one day turn on us in the most horrific of ways. The Internet will grow up to be Skynet. In the meantime, we make fun of Google while we still can. ◆

"O.K., just tell me, which college classmate did you Google today?"

BARBARA SMALLER, APRIL 23, 2012

*"Please understand. I don't sell access to the government.
I merely sell access to the guys who do sell access to the government."*

*"The only solution I can see is to hold a series of long and
costly hearings in order to put off finding a solution."*

TOP ED FISHER, JULY 7, 1986   BOTTOM JACK ZIEGLER, JUNE 12, 2000

"What about business—which branch is that?"

"I keep my core beliefs written on my palm for easy reference."

TOP DAVID SIPRESS, JANUARY 31, 2011   BOTTOM FRANK COTHAM, MAY 18, 1998

*"No, I didn't. I never said there should be
no government regulation."*

"Leak this against my wishes."

*"I don't think you can distance yourself from the
White House on this one. After all, you are the president."*

TOP CHARLES BARSOTTI, FEBRUARY 9, 2004   MIDDLE DAVID SIPRESS, NOVEMBER 10, 2003   BOTTOM ARNIE LEVIN, DECEMBER 1, 1997

"I have a brief statement, a clarification, and two denials."

PETER STEINER, FEBRUARY 22, 1993

"Let's change 'brink of chaos' to 'everything is wonderful.'"

"The mark of true leadership is knowing when to resign in disgrace."

TOP DAVID SIPRESS, OCTOBER 18, 2004   BOTTOM CHRISTOPHER WEYANT, SEPTEMBER 26, 2005

*SEE ALSO ELECTIONS, JUDGES, POLITICIANS

*"You can't please all the people all the time,
so you might as well please the pharmaceutical lobby."*

"It's always cozy in here. We're insulated by layers of bureaucracy."

TOP BARBARA SMALLER, JUNE 12, 2006   BOTTOM FRANK COTHAM, MARCH 17, 1997

G.P.S. FOR GUYS

"Recalculating route."

TOP MICK STEVENS, JANUARY 17, 2011   BOTTOM ROBERT LEIGHTON, DECEMBER 20, 2010

"Until there's a reason not to trust the G.P.S., I'm trusting the G.P.S."

"Sorry, still rerouting."

TOP MICHAEL MASLIN, JANUARY 5, 2015   BOTTOM PAUL NOTH, JANUARY 2, 2017

"*Recalculating…recalculating…*"

DAVID SIPRESS, APRIL 4, 2011

"Why didn't you spring for a proper G.P.S.?"

TOP ROZ CHAST, OCTOBER 11, 2010 BOTTOM P.C. VEY, DECEMBER 22, 2008

"My fellow graduates, today we leave behind the trappings of youth, step boldly onto the road of life, and move back in with our parents."

"I know so much that I don't know where to begin."

TOP DAVID SIPRESS, MAY 28, 2012   BOTTOM JAMES STEVENSON, JUNE 1, 1987

*"Congratulations, keep moving, please.
Congratulations, keep moving, please. Congratulations . . ."*

"Sometimes I think we want this more than he does."

TOP BARNEY TOBEY, JUNE 10, 1974   BOTTOM KIM WARP, MAY 12, 2014

"What does he know, and how long will he know it?"

"I didn't know you had a minor."

TOP FRANK COTHAM, MAY 27, 2002   BOTTOM LIANA FINCK, NOVEMBER 23, 2015

TOP BRUCE KAPLAN, MAY 18, 1992   BOTTOM ROZ CHAST, MAY 30, 2011

"Sorry, but I'm going to have to issue you a summons
for reckless grammar and driving without an apostrophe."

"What can I say? I was an English major."

TOP MICHAEL MASLIN, SEPTEMBER 7, 1987   BOTTOM J.C. DUFFY, JULY 28, 2008

"*You don't need to sacrifice good grammar in order to talk dirty.*"

"*Please! Pardon the dangling participle.*"

TOP ZACHARY KANIN, MAY 25, 2009   BOTTOM EDWARD KOREN, APRIL 29, 1985

"'I' before 'e,' except after 'c.'"   *"Drop dead!"*

"Whom? Meem?"

TOP LEE LORENZ, MAY 13, 1974 BOTTOM LEE LORENZ, JULY 7, 1975

*SEE ALSO CROSSWORDS, QUOTATIONS

"And remember—no more subjunctives where the correct mood is indicative."

PETER STEINER, JANUARY 22, 2001

"Hey, good-lookin', whatcha got cookin'?"

"Mercury, Mars, this is the bitch goddess Success."

TOP TON SMITS, OCTOBER 7, 1972   BOTTOM DANA FRADON, MARCH 22, 1993

"If you're so good, why can't you ever strike twice in the same place?"

TOP CHARLES ADDAMS, AUGUST 15, 1936   BOTTOM MISCHA RICHTER, SEPTEMBER 23, 1967

EDWARD FRASCINO, JULY 31, 1989

"The Icarus story is just that—a story."

"Now I've seen everything."

TOP VICTORIA ROBERTS, APRIL 26, 1993   MIDDLE MISCHA RICHTER, MARCH 7, 1964   BOTTOM ANATOL KOVARSKY, MAY 1, 1954

"His rates just went up again and the service is still lousy."

"He came with the pool."

TOP ED FISHER, APRIL 7, 1973   BOTTOM WHITNEY DARROW, JR., JUNE 13, 1964

"Achilles! How's the wife? The kids? The heel?"

"Keep working on it. I like the concept, but it lacks scope."

TOP DANA FRADON, FEBRUARY 6, 1989   BOTTOM ROWLAND WILSON, DECEMBER 30, 1961

"Love your work."

"Don't panic. I'm just a sore throat."

TOP MATTHEW DIFFEE, DECEMBER 26, 2005   BOTTOM SIDNEY HARRIS, JANUARY 5, 1976

"Thank goodness you're here—
I can't accomplish anything unless I have a deadline."

"Relax, honey—change is good."

TOP DAVID SIPRESS, DECEMBER 20, 2004   BOTTOM BOB MANKOFF, APRIL 19, 1993

TIME'S UP

T HE PERSONIFICATION OF DEATH as a cloaked man or a skeleton carrying a scythe has long been a staple of apocalyptic illustration and editorial cartooning. Historically, the Grim Reaper was indeed grim, but in *The New Yorker,* where he first appeared in the late nineteen-sixties, the scenario is far from tragic. That's because the cartoonists have transformed him. To start with, he's not really a symbol of death anymore. We are no longer in the land of pestilence and famine but in an America of ambition, leisure time, consumerism, and hypochondria. Cartoonists, then, see the Grim Reaper not as an alien presence but as one of us. They start to ask questions like, **"Just what kind of life does Death have, anyway?"** Maybe he's just a working stiff working with stiffs. ♦

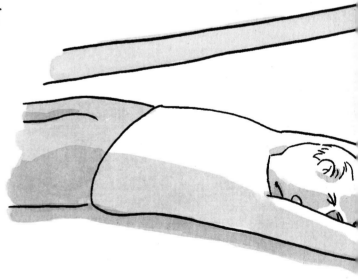

Kanin

ZACHARY KANIN, DECEMBER 15, 2008

"Hey, don't I get a receipt?"

TOP MICK STEVENS, NOVEMBER 18, 2002   BOTTOM ARNIE LEVIN, JANUARY 16, 1995

*SEE ALSO DOOMSAYERS, FUNERALS, TOMBSTONES

A LOOK AHEAD

GOOD NEWS/ BAD NEWS

TOP ROZ CHAST, AUGUST 6, 2001   BOTTOM J.C. DUFFY, APRIL 19, 2010

"Shadow, nothing. I saw Elvis."

"Louie went outside the other day and saw his shadow.
We're in for a long, hard winter."

TOP DANNY SHANAHAN, FEBRUARY 4, 1991   BOTTOM JAMES MULLIGAN, NOVEMBER 18, 1972

"Have we got one that says 'Happy Groundhog Day'?"

WHITNEY DARROW, JR., JANUARY 31, 1970

*"Does the 'Times' say anything about this ground hog
in New Jersey that came out of his hole and climbed a tree?"*

TOP EVERETT OPIE, FEBRUARY 3, 1962 BOTTOM PERRY BARLOW, FEBRUARY 5, 1938

*"As you can see, ladies and gentlemen, the available
data clearly suggest six more weeks of winter."*

"I saw my shadow. It made me look fat."

TOP JOHN CALDWELL, FEBRUARY 4, 2002   BOTTOM LEO CULLUM, FEBRUARY 7, 2005

"And on my right is Joe Nast, representing an opposing viewpoint."

"O.K., but let's say you have up to six hundred intruders per minute."

TOP EDWARD KOREN, AUGUST 8, 1983   BOTTOM MATTHEW DIFFEE, SEPTEMBER 5, 2011

"Figured I better get one before they crack down on the tank shows."

"What kind of mischief are you into now?"

TOP LARRY TREPEL, SEPTEMBER 30, 2013   BOTTOM SAM GROSS, JUNE 13, 1994

"As a matter of fact, you did catch us at a bad time."

"My first choice, of course, is to solve things amicably."

TOP BOB MANKOFF, JANUARY 30, 1995   BOTTOM MIKE TWOHY, NOVEMBER 15, 2004

"*Still, I hope you won't give up barking entirely.*"

"*What the hell was I <u>supposed</u> to do? I've been declawed!*"

TOP FRANK COTHAM, MARCH 27, 2006   BOTTOM FRANK GOTHAM, OCTOBER 9, 1995

HAIR

HANSEL & GRETEL

HAPPINESS

HEAT WAVES

HEAVEN

HIPPIES

HITLER

HOBBIES

HOLIDAYS

HOLLYWOOD

HONEY, I'M HOME

HORSE COSTUME

HORSES

HOURGLASSES

HUMPTY DUMPTY

"I see he finally got rid of that idiotic comb-over."

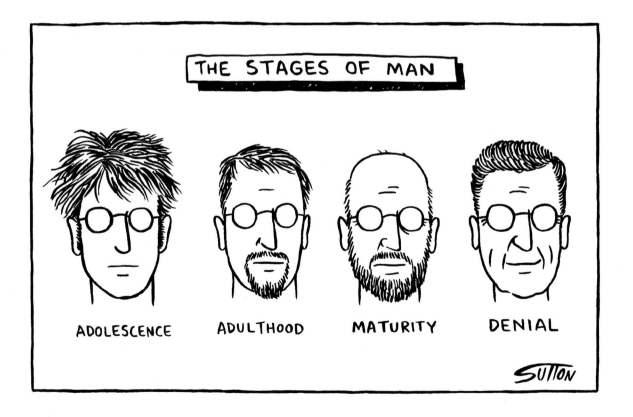

TOP JACK ZIEGLER, MARCH 16, 2009   BOTTOM WARD SUTTON, OCTOBER 22, 2007

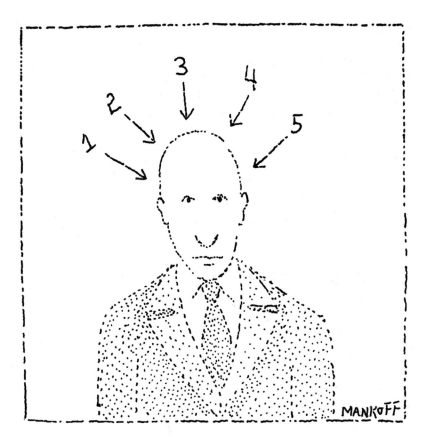

The Five Major Warning Signs of Baldness

"I love it. Who did it?"

TOP BOB MANKOFF, AUGUST 13, 1979 BOTTOM CHARLES BARSOTTI, NOVEMBER 7, 1994

"It's a Calatrava."

"I can't find that much hair in a drain and not see stress issues."

TOP STEVE DUENES, OCTOBER 30, 2006   BOTTOM JULIA SUITS, MARCH 3, 2008

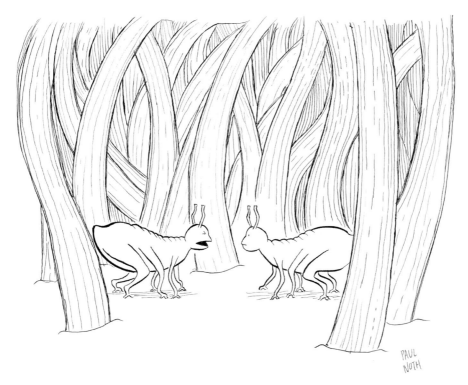

"*What I'm about to tell you does not leave this mustache.*"

"*I don't know about hair care, Rapunzel, but I'm thinking a good cream rinse plus protein conditioner might just solve both our problems.*"

TOP PAUL NOTH, MARCH 17, 2008 BOTTOM MICHAEL MASLIN, APRIL 10, 2000

*"I'm looking for a nice cottage in a wooded area
that would appeal to children in the four-to-seven age group."*

"We'll catch 'em and cook 'em when the sugar wears off."

TOP BERNARD SCHOENBAUM, NOVEMBER 1, 1999   BOTTOM HARRY BLISS, NOVEMBER 3, 2003

"This whole forest is getting unbearably gentrified."

TOP JAMES STEVENSON, JULY 4, 1988   BOTTOM DANNY SHANAHAN, FEBRUARY 25, 2008

"Remember when we used to have to fatten the kids up first?"

TOP BERNARD SCHOENBAUM, JULY 25, 1994 BOTTOM CHRISTOPHER WEYANT, DECEMBER 22, 2003

*SEE ALSO ARCHITECTURE, CINDERELLA, DIET

TOP LEE LORENZ, JUNE 13, 1977   BOTTOM ARNIE LEVIN, MAY 22, 2000

"I can't wait to grow up and be happy."

"Have you ever tried buying lots of stuff?"

TOP ROBERT WEBER, JUNE 3, 1991   BOTTOM MATTHEW DIFFEE, MAY 18, 2009

*"I roamed the world trying to find myself, and then I came home
and discovered happiness right here in my own back yard."*

RICHARD TAYLOR, SEPTEMBER 14, 1957

"Am I a happy man or just an asymptomatic one?"

"This lovely car has not brought us happiness. You agree, Morris?
That is why I am now thinking in terms of having the entire house recarpeted."

TOP BARBARA SMALLER, MAY 4, 2009   BOTTOM J.B. HANDELSMAN, JULY 26, 1969

*SEE ALSO BLUEBIRD OF HAPPINESS, LAUGHTER, SMILEY FACE

"Oh-oh! Look who's back!"

"I need to wait until the euphoria wears off before I start dating again."

TOP BORIS DRUCKER, JANUARY 14, 1991 BOTTOM DREW DERNAVICH, MAY 26, 2008

"These days, I suppose, air-conditioning breakdown
must be regarded as one of the facts of life."

"Shall I compare thee to a summer's day?"

TOP HENRY MARTIN, JULY 1, 1972   BOTTOM DAVID SIPRESS, AUGUST 21, 2006

"Hot enough for you, Mr. Cadwalader?"

TOP LIZA DONNELLY, AUGUST 7, 1995   BOTTOM HENRY MARTIN, JULY 13, 1981

THE CONCRETE CAFÉ

"A word to the wise, Lucille. Only mad dogs and Englishmen
go out in the midday sun. One lump or two?"

TOP ROZ CHAST, AUGUST 21, 2000   BOTTOM GEORGE BOOTH, AUGUST 11, 1980

"Consider yourself chased."

TOP GEORGE PRICE, JULY 10, 1954   BOTTOM CHARLES BARSOTTI, JULY 12, 1999

"Oh, eternal life is fine, but what I really like is
getting to wear flip-flops all the time."

"Wings that don't work! Harps we can't play!
And these infuriating nighties! Are you sure this isn't Hell?"

TOP BOB MANKOFF, AUGUST 4, 2003   BOTTOM JACK ZIEGLER, DECEMBER 10, 2001

"*For goodness' sake, rest in <u>peace</u>!*"

"*Two bars—how about you?*"

TOP AL ROSS, SEPTEMBER 11, 1995   BOTTOM ALEX GREGORY, DECEMBER 13, 2010

THE AFTER-AFTER-PARTY

THE VERY THOUGHT of Heaven ignites our hopes and fears—mostly the hope that we will get in and the fear that we won't. With such built-in tension, it is no surprise that cartoonists keep mining Heaven for material. Working with the same props and scenery—wings, halos, robes, puffy cloudscapes, pearly gates—cartoonists have drawn endless varieties of paradise. Some shine for their "Superb Martinis!"; others are marred by a single imperfection that threatens to vex us for eternity. And still others are simply a letdown: the wings are made of paper, the robes are hotel surplus, and the Wi-Fi is spotty. **It is odd that pondering Heaven produces so much anxiety.** Pondering Hell, on the other hand, is simply a gleeful enterprise. Maybe this is because we think of it as a place reserved only for other people. Or maybe we figure that, if this is where we're headed (no doubt for being so judgmental of others), we had better enjoy a few laughs along the way. ♦

Kanin

ZACHARY KANIN, MARCH 15, 2010

"I always thought the heavenly gates would be pearly, not golden."

*"This is a little embarrassing to admit, but everything
that happens happens for no real reason."*

TOP HENRY MARTIN, SEPTEMBER 10, 1990   BOTTOM BRUCE KAPLAN, MAY 29, 2000

*SEE ALSO SAINT PETER

"Does anyone else's robe say 'Hyatt'?"

*"And twelve: How did you learn about us?—
(a) church, (b) synagogue, (c) family member, (d) word of mouth?"*

TOP MATTHEW DIFFEE, OCTOBER 3, 2005   BOTTOM HENRY MARTIN, DECEMBER 15, 1997

"I mean, like, you know, I never dreamed I would ever
say this to anyone, but would you get a haircut, Larry?"

"I mean, like, Son, when you're in your teens and doing your own thing,
you'll still dig me and we'll always groove with one another, right?"

TOP WARREN MILLER, AUGUST 31, 1968   BOTTOM WARREN MILLER, MAY 4, 1968

"It's about a little locomotive that says, like, 'Why should I?'"

TOP DONALD REILLY, JUNE 8, 1968   BOTTOM ROZ CHAST, MAY 11, 1998

"Where have we failed?"

*"Hello, me in 1990. I suppose by now you are making
piles of bread and going reactionary, so let me remind you…"*

TOP ROBERT WEBER, MAY 11, 1968 BOTTOM WILLIAM O'BRIAN, NOVEMBER 2, 1968

*SEE ALSO BEATNIKS, HAIR, PEACE

BOB MANKOFF, AUGUST 20, 1979

"*I think I may say, without fear of contradiction…*"

"*Oh, no! You're the real one.*"

TOP CARL ROSE, APRIL 25, 1942   BOTTOM ALAIN, OCTOBER 28, 1944

Dreams of Glory

TOP WILLIAM STEIG, FEBRUARY 19, 1944   BOTTOM MISCHA RICHTER, NOVEMBER 18, 1944

JOHN GROTH, JANUARY 18, 1941

Hitler's Bunker

"…and as for those postwar trials, we can always plead insanity."

TOP SAUL STEINBERG, MARCH 29, 1947   BOTTOM CARL ROSE, AUGUST 14, 1943

"Please, sir, you must help me! I'll be sixty-five next
week and I have no one else to turn to."

"I'm looking for an outside interest I can do from my couch."

TOP WHITNEY DARROW, JR., MAY 15, 1971   BOTTOM BARBARA SMALLER, JANUARY 12, 2004

"Thursdays and Saturdays, it's glassblowing,
Mondays and Wednesdays it's Morris dancing!"

"Jeffrey makes all our furniture himself."

TOP GEORGE BOOTH, JUNE 12, 2000   BOTTOM BOB MANKOFF, FEBRUARY 19, 1990

"Agnes, you know very well I'm not interested in rose-breasted grosbeaks and rose-breasted grosbeaks aren't interested in me."

"You know, Margaret, a lot of people who can knit don't."

TOP STAN HUNT, SEPTEMBER 28, 1963 BOTTOM VICTORIA ROBERTS, FEBRUARY 17, 2003

*"Mr. Cartwright says you have to make a career decision—
African violets or accounting."*

TOP JACK ZIEGLER, DECEMBER 18, 2000 BOTTOM HENRY MARTIN, OCTOBER 15, 1990

"Sometimes I don't read my mail."

"We'd like to promote the concept of a nontraditional Thanksgiving."

TOP VICTORIA ROBERTS, DECEMBER 18, 2000   BOTTOM LEO CULLUM, NOVEMBER 29, 1993

MANKOFF

*"We've agreed, then, to deck the halls,
but the resolution to be jolly has been tabled."*

*"My family likes to set up our grudges at Thanksgiving,
stew over them through December, then take our revenge at Christmas."*

TOP BOB MANKOFF, DECEMBER 4, 1989 BOTTOM BARBARA SMALLER, NOVEMBER 22, 2004

JANUARY 3RD AT ROCKEFELLER CENTER

JACK ZIEGLER, JANUARY 10, 1994

"I'm afraid I've got some bad news."

TOP ROZ CHAST, DECEMBER 10, 2007 BOTTOM DANNY SHANAHAN, NOVEMBER 3, 1997

"*The knees are the first to go.*"

"*A lot of it is just legal mumbo-jumbo.*"

TOP DANNY SHANAHAN, DECEMBER 28, 1992   MIDDLE MIKE TWOHY, AUGUST 25, 1997   BOTTOM ARNIE LEVIN, JANUARY 2, 1989

*SEE ALSO EASTER BUNNY, VALENTINES

*"They say we can go there for Thanksgiving
or they can cut us out of the will. Our choice."*

TOP ROZ CHAST, NOVEMBER 1, 1993 BOTTOM DAVID SIPRESS, NOVEMBER 19, 2001

"I think you'll like this idea—it's sort of 'dull' meets 'inoffensive.'"

"Let's remake an old classic with worse everything!"

TOP BRUCE KAPLAN, NOVEMBER 1, 1999   BOTTOM MIKE TWOHY, SEPTEMBER 29, 2008

"*I just don't think a giant flaming blob of alien ectoplasm would say that.*"

"*It's basically the 'Tragedy of King Lear' but with animated penguins.*"

TOP ALEX GREGORY, MAY 29, 2000   BOTTOM BOB MANKOFF, MAY 14, 2007

THAT'S ENTERTAINMENT

T HE SUNSHINE, THE CELEBRITIES, the glitz, the glamour—ah, Tinseltown. What's not to loathe? Much like Woody Allen's character in "Annie Hall," cartoonists for *The New Yorker* harbor a reflexive distrust of Hollywood's charm. Surely there's something suspicious, if not downright sinister, about a culture in which an elephant says to a casting agent, "I can also play a hippo." (Leo Cullum, a former resident of Malibu, drew that gag in the belly of the bedazzled beast.) Regional rivalry certainly fuels the jousting. New York City begrudges Los Angeles its climate, while Los Angeles begrudges New York City its transit. But the barbs that are lobbed across flyover country reveal a kinship between the coasts. After all, the classic film-biz pitch **"It's this movie meets that movie"** describes cartooning in a nutshell: the surprising synthesis of opposites. Several artists from *The New Yorker's* stable—including Bruce Kaplan, Alex Gregory, and Zachary Kanin—have even made hay in Hollywood. Others, like William Haefeli and Matthew Diffee, call L.A. home. And the rest, if not bicoastal, are at least bi-curious. Is life in the City of Angels really so heavenly? And, more important, can a person reapply sunscreen every half hour and remain sane? ◆

PETER STEINER, APRIL 1, 1996

"No movie deal yet, but Kinko's is extremely interested in the idea of making multiple copies of your screenplay."

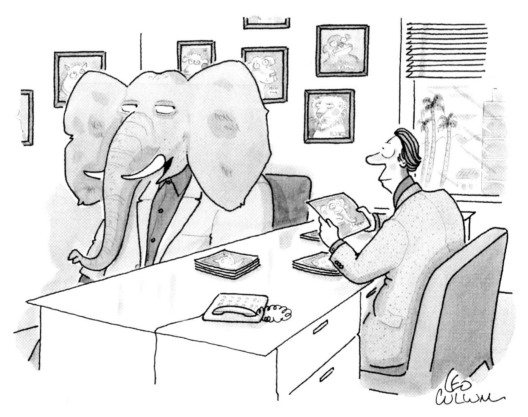

"I can also play a hippo."

TOP DREW DERNAVICH, OCTOBER 20, 2003   BOTTOM LEO CULLUM, JULY 23, 2007

"We've been married a long time in Hollywood years."

"Call my attorney and say that I killed Ted in self-defense.
Call my publicist and say that I wish Ted the best of luck in all his future endeavors."

TOP FRANK COTHAM, MARCH 6, 2000   BOTTOM ALEX GREGORY, JANUARY 9, 2006

"Honey, I'm home."

"Honey, I'm home."

TOP SAM GROSS, JANUARY 27, 1992   BOTTOM MICK STEVENS, JUNE 27, 1988

"Honey, I'm home."

"Honey, I'm home."

TOP JACK ZIEGLER, OCTOBER 13, 1997 BOTTOM LEE LORENZ, MAY 19, 2003

"Honey, am I home?"

"Sweetheart, I'm ho—"

TOP FRANK COTHAM, OCTOBER 10, 1994   BOTTOM TOM CHENEY, MARCH 11, 2002

"Honey—I'm paroled!"

TOP MICK STEVENS, JUNE 26, 1989   BOTTOM MICHAEL MASLIN, JUNE 2, 1997

PAUL
NOTH

"Will he know what this is regarding?"

"Want a blind date after the show?"

TOP PAUL NOTH, APRIL 21, 2008   BOTTOM GARRETT PRICE, AUGUST 19, 1939

*"As children aren't an issue in this marriage,
may I suggest that you consider staying together for the sake of the horse?"*

"We're watching television less and making our own fun more."

TOP MICHAEL MASLIN, APRIL 22, 1996   BOTTOM VICTORIA ROBERTS, MARCH 20, 2006

TOP JACK ZIEGLER, JUNE 10, 1991   BOTTOM SAM COBEAN, DECEMBER 2, 1950

"Is there a doctor in the audience?"

TOP ROBERT DAY, NOVEMBER 8, 1941   BOTTOM RICHARD DECKER, JANUARY 28, 1933

UNWISE INVESTMENTS

Stumblebum

SIRED BY: CLUMSY OAF
OUT OF: LADY UH-OH

Galloping Consumption

SIRED BY: MISTER PROUST
OUT OF: PENICILLIN

Molasses in January

SIRED BY: BUMP ON A LOG
OUT OF: JUST DOZING

R. Chast

"I just know I'm going to love horses all my life.
That's why I'm planning to have a career in banking, insurance, and real estate."

TOP ROZ CHAST, NOVEMBER 19, 1984   BOTTOM WARREN MILLER, MAY 9, 1988

"Over, damn you, over!"

"Really, only you can tell yourself to giddyup."

TOP ZACHARY KANIN, NOVEMBER 7, 2011   BOTTOM BRUCE KAPLAN, MARCH 31, 2003

"Must be a celebrity inside!"

"If you kick her with the left spur, she'll give you more lumbar support."

TOP MICHAEL MASLIN, OCTOBER 24, 2011 BOTTOM DREW DERNAVICH, FEBRUARY 14, 2005

*SEE ALSO CENTAURS, COWBOYS, TROJAN HORSE

"You keep saying, 'Whoa, Nellie.' My name is Todd."

"…and please make me a better horsewoman. Amen."

TOP MICHAEL MASLIN, SEPTEMBER 19, 2011   BOTTOM MARY PETTY, OCTOBER 18, 1947

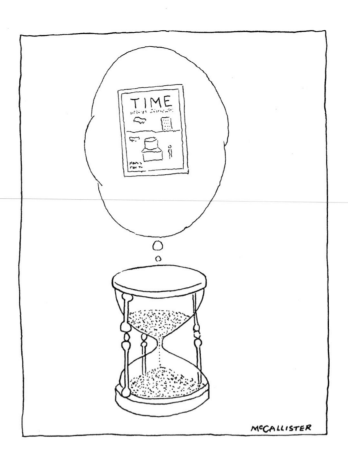

TOP RICHARD McCALLISTER, AUGUST 13, 1979 BOTTOM TOM CHENEY, AUGUST 11, 2003

"What a pleasure to find someone else who detests digital watches."

"Well, I see my time's about up."

TOP EDWARD KOREN, FEBRUARY 9, 1981 BOTTOM AL ROSS, SEPTEMBER 14, 1963

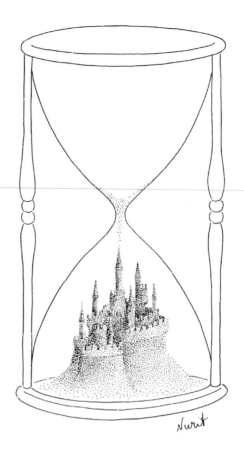

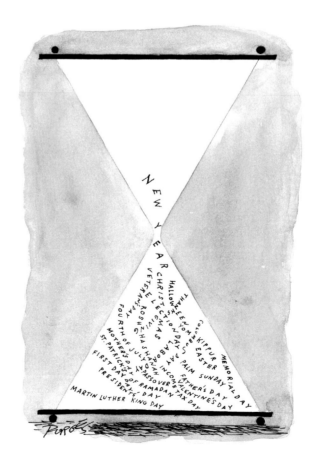

TOP NURIT KARLIN, MAY 1, 1978   BOTTOM PETER PORGES, JANUARY 5, 1998

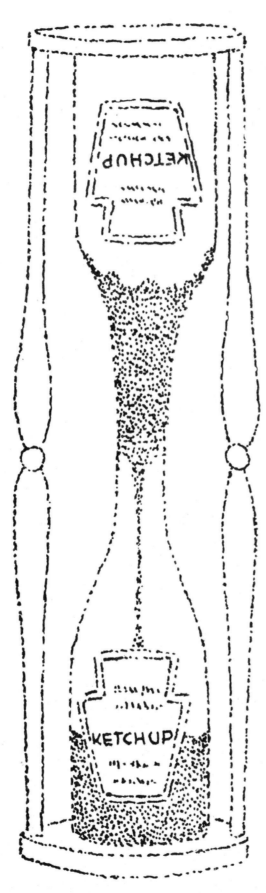

MANKOFF

BOB MANKOFF, FEBRUARY 25, 1980

H

"I did all my own stunts."

"I'm afraid you have only three minutes to live."

TOP ALEX GREGORY, JUNE 6, 2005   BOTTOM ARNIE LEVIN, JUNE 22, 1992

"You know what? I probably could have put Humpty Dumpty
back together again but I was just too pissed."

"Eventually, I'd like to see you able to put <u>yourself</u> back together."

TOP BRUCE KAPLAN, OCTOBER 4, 2010   BOTTOM LEO CULLUM, MAY 22, 2006

"First, we need to stabilize his spine!"

"He's in an H.M.O. Get some of the King's horses and a few of the King's men."

TOP DANNY SHANAHAN, DECEMBER 22, 2008   BOTTOM LEO CULLUM, APRIL 1, 1996

*SEE ALSO BEDTIME STORIES, THREE LITTLE PIGS, TORTOISE & THE HARE

"Maybe they didn't try hard enough."

"Funny—all the king's horses don't seem to be helping at all."

TOP AL ROSS, JUNE 21, 1993   BOTTOM ZACHARY KANIN, SEPTEMBER 22, 2008

FRANK MODELL, FEBRUARY 21, 1959

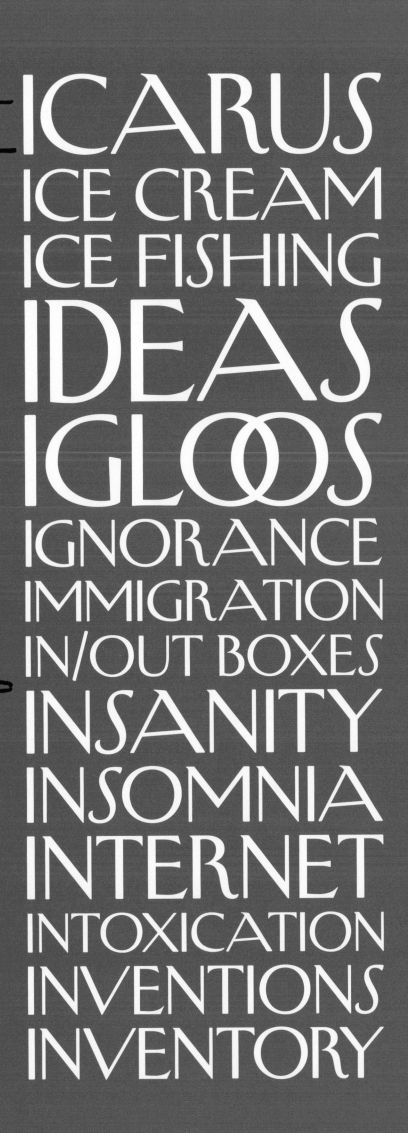

ICARUS
ICE CREAM
ICE FISHING
IDEAS
IGLOOS
IGNORANCE
IMMIGRATION
IN/OUT BOXES
INSANITY
INSOMNIA
INTERNET
INTOXICATION
INVENTIONS
INVENTORY

"Why do you automatically assume that I'll fly too close to the sun?"

*"Well, maybe it won't work,
but somebody has to start the ball rolling!"*

TOP BRUCE KAPLAN, AUGUST 6, 2001 BOTTOM ROBERT WEBER, SEPTEMBER 7, 1963

"*I'm afraid he hasn't given sufficient thought
to the problem of reëntry.*"

CROSSED PATHS

Icarus Meets the Ancient Mariner

TOP NOEL WATSON, NOVEMBER 21, 1970   BOTTOM RONALD SEARLE, MARCH 9, 1992

"Pecan pie with rum-raisin ice cream is the best revenge."

TOP SAM COBEAN, JULY 24, 1948   BOTTOM ROBERT WEBER, FEBRUARY 26, 1990

"It's true, Darlene—until I met Ben
I didn't care if my cone was sugar or wafer."

"Fresh sprinkles for your ice cream?"

TOP MICHAEL MASLIN, SEPTEMBER 16, 1991   BOTTOM SIDNEY HARRIS, MAY 18, 1992

"Pistachio almond—that's the buyout."

TOP CHARLES BARSOTTI, JANUARY 26, 2009 BOTTOM JACK ZIEGLER, JUNE 26, 2006

*"I could double-check, sir, but I believe the last of the
coconut frozen-fruit bars now rests in your hand."*

TOP JACK ZIEGLER, JULY 7, 1997 BOTTOM MICHAEL MASLIN, JANUARY 9, 1989

"Who <u>asked</u> you to share my interests?"

ICE FLY-FISHING WITH DOUG

TOP GEORGE PRICE, DECEMBER 18, 1954   BOTTOM MICHAEL CRAWFORD, JANUARY 23, 2006

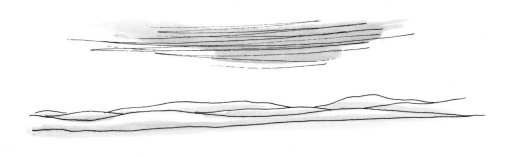

ICE WHALING

TOP MATTHEW DIFFEE, NOVEMBER 2, 2009 BOTTOM MICK STEVENS, MARCH 24, 2003

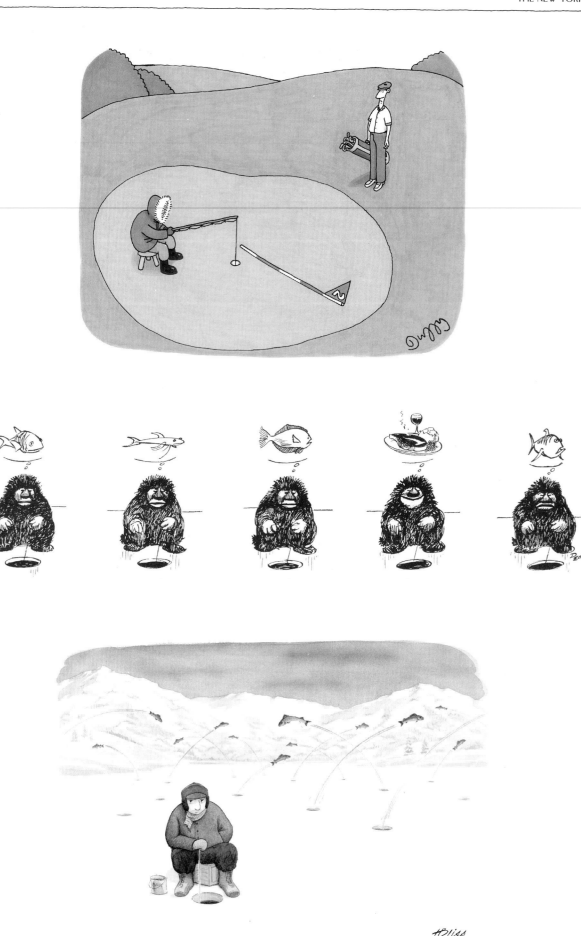

TOP J.C. DUFFY, JULY 3, 2006   MIDDLE ELDON DEDINI, MARCH 14, 1964   BOTTOM HARRY BLISS, FEBRUARY 19, 2001

GIDEON AMICHAY, JANUARY 16, 1995

"Well, Stoddard, I think I've bounced enough ideas off you for one day."

WHERE EARL GETS HIS IDEAS

TOP LEO CULLUM, APRIL 26, 1993 BOTTOM MICHAEL CRAWFORD, MARCH 9, 1992

"Damn it, gentlemen, these are medieval times.
They demand medieval ideas."

"For all his brilliance, we're going to have to replace Trewell.
He never quite seems able to reduce his ideas to football analogies."

TOP JACK ZIEGLER, MAY 26, 2003   BOTTOM ED FISHER, MARCH 11, 1991

"I've asked you all here today to help me develop some really stupid ideas."

"I get my best ideas in airports, peeking at other people's laptops."

TOP ED FISHER, OCTOBER 24, 1994   BOTTOM FRANK COTHAM, OCTOBER 10, 2005

*SEE ALSO INVENTIONS, LIGHT BULB IDEA, QUESTIONS

"Just how fresh are these insights?"

"Where does he get all his ideas?"

TOP LEE LORENZ, SEPTEMBER 24, 1984   BOTTOM BRUCE KAPLAN, OCTOBER 17, 2005

"Didn't you hear it? A sort of crunch."

TOP ROBERT DAY, SEPTEMBER 30, 1961   BOTTOM ALAIN, OCTOBER 15, 1955

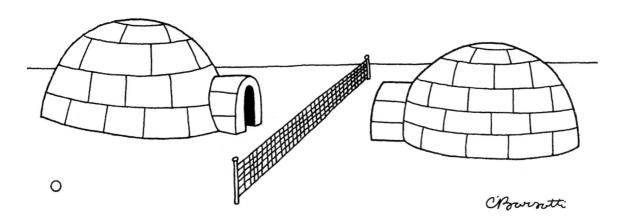

"*Serve again—I wasn't ready.*"

"*If it didn't sound so crazy, I'd say I was seasick.*"

TOP CHARLES BARSOTTI, MARCH 3, 2003   MIDDLE CHARLES ADDAMS, DECEMBER 4, 1971   BOTTOM MISCHA RICHTER, APRIL 27, 1968

"Will a dollar help?"

TOP NICK DOWNES, SEPTEMBER 21, 1998   BOTTOM ROBERT WEBER, JANUARY 6, 1992

594

"Aunt Claire asked you a question dear.
Are you the pitcher or the catcher?"

"The earth is flat. Pass it on."

TOP PERRY BARLOW, JUNE 19, 1954   BOTTOM WARREN MILLER, AUGUST 27, 1966

"'Ignorance of the law is no excuse.' Golly!
I never heard that one! Did you ever hear that one?"

"I never can remember.
Is it Manet or Monet who isn't
as good as the others?"

"What'll I do with it now?"

TOP WARREN MILLER, MAY 20, 1974   MIDDLE CHARLES SAXON, APRIL 6, 1968   BOTTOM PETER ARNO, AUGUST 24, 1929

"On the other hand, the sand I'm burying
my head in is in Amagansett."

"Frankly, I'm worried about the country.
Our questions on substantive issues have been getting
one-hundred-per-cent 'Don't know.'"

TOP LEO CULLUM, AUGUST 6, 2007   BOTTOM JAMES STEVENSON, OCTOBER 6, 1975

"Well, they look pretty undocumented to me."

"On my home planet, I was a deity."

TOP J.B. HANDELSMAN, APRIL 10, 2006   BOTTOM EMILY FLAKE, APRIL 22, 2013

"The country grandpa came from was a stinking hellhole of unspeakable poverty where everyone was always happy."

"You fellas need a job?"

TOP DAVID SIPRESS, JANUARY 24, 2000   BOTTOM JASON PATTERSON, NOVEMBER 13, 2006

*"All right, folks, we'll be landing in a few minutes. You first-class passengers gather
on my left. You huddled masses and wretched refuse gather on my right."*

WILLIAM O'BRIAN, MARCH 17, 1973

600

"We're just here for a few days to get our names crudely Anglicized, do some shopping, sightseeing—stuff like that."

"And yet <u>another</u> headache for the Immigration and Naturalization Service!"

TOP MICHAEL CRAWFORD, OCTOBER 13, 2014   BOTTOM DANA FRADON, JUNE 22, 1992

"In America, the streets are paved with gold.
And everything else is stuffed with cheese and bacon."

"Anything you say with an accent may be used against you."

TOP BENJAMIN SCHWARTZ, MARCH 16, 2015   BOTTOM PAUL NOTH, SEPTEMBER 20, 2010

"I guess the Garcías won't be coming to visit anymore."

"What's our immigration policy?"

TOP FRANK COTHAM, APRIL 24, 2006 BOTTOM ROBERT WEBER, DECEMBER 15, 1997

SIPRESS

TOP DAVID SIPRESS, FEBRUARY 11, 2002   BOTTOM FARLEY KATZ, DECEMBER 13, 2010

TOP ROZ CHAST, OCTOBER 28, 2002   BOTTOM BOB MANKOFF, SEPTEMBER 30, 2002

TOP ARNIE LEVIN, JULY 27, 1998 BOTTOM DAVID SIPRESS, APRIL 2, 2001

*SEE ALSO OFFICE LIFE, WATER COOLER, WHILE YOU WERE OUT

TOP DAVID SIPRESS, JULY 26, 2010 BOTTOM RICHARD CLINE, JANUARY 8, 1996

"You can't expect to get back to normal if you never <u>were</u> normal."

"Bad news—we're all out of our minds.
You're going to have to be the lone healthy person in this family."

TOP MICK STEVENS, NOVEMBER 12, 2001   BOTTOM BRUCE KAPLAN, DECEMBER 21, 1998

"Mr. Stewart is out of his gourd at the moment. May I take a message?"

"Of course you're not going crazy. That man over there is <u>also</u> fretting over the plight of the platypus."

TOP CLAUDE SMITH, FEBRUARY 1, 1964   BOTTOM HARRY BLISS, DECEMBER 23, 2002

"My voices told me to just relax today!"

"Oh, by the way, sweetheart, I thought I should tell you.
I've decided to leave the mainstream and join the lunatic fringe."

TOP GEORGE BOOTH, JANUARY 28, 2002   BOTTOM JACK ZIEGLER, AUGUST 18, 1975

"Crazy bastard thinks he's Napoleon."

FRANK COTHAM, MARCH 27, 2000

*"If you were slipping inexorably into psychosis,
you'd tell me, wouldn't you?"*

"I don't know how you do it. If I had your job, I'd go nuts."

TOP WILLIAM HAEFELI, MARCH 9, 1998 BOTTOM BOB MANKOFF, JANUARY 27, 1997

"I couldn't sleep."

"That concludes our broadcast day. Go to bed."

TOP MICHAEL CRAWFORD, SEPTEMBER 14, 1992 BOTTOM CHARLES BARSOTTI, FEBRUARY 7, 1977

"All right, but promise you'll come in and go to bed the instant you do discover the meaning of it all."

BARNEY TOBEY, SEPTEMBER 9, 1972

"What do you do when you can't sleep?"

*"When I can't sleep, I find that it sometimes helps
to get up and jot down my anxieties."*

TOP PETER STEINER, MARCH 24, 2003   BOTTOM DREW DERNAVICH, JUNE 9, 2008

*SEE ALSO BEDTIME STORIES, DREAMS, OWLS

"How can you just lie there and <u>accept</u> continental drift?"

TOP CHARLES ADDAMS, JULY 3, 1978   BOTTOM DANNY SHANAHAN, MARCH 27, 2000

*"Excuse me, I'm lost.
Can you direct me to the information superhighway?"*

*"We need to rethink our strategy of hoping
the Internet will just go away."*

TOP WARREN MILLER, JANUARY 31, 1994   BOTTOM TOM TORO, MAY 5, 2014

"On the Internet, nobody knows you're a dog."

*"It's very important that you try very, very hard to remember
where you electronically transferred Mommy and Daddy's assets."*

TOP PETER STEINER, JULY 5, 1993   BOTTOM MICHAEL MASLIN, JULY 24, 2000

*"I got my ticket for three dollars over the Internet.
Are you going to eat that salmon?"*

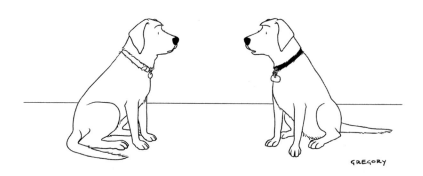

*"I had my own blog for a while, but I decided to go back
to just pointless, incessant barking."*

"Didn't I see you on YouTube riding a Roomba?"

TOP LEO CULLUM, APRIL 17, 2000   MIDDLE ALEX GREGORY, SEPTEMBER 12, 2005   BOTTOM SHANNON WHEELER, MAY 4, 2009

DAVID SIPRESS, SEPTEMBER 22, 2014

VIRTUAL INSANITY

Cartoons lampoon life, and life has moved online. But once upon a time, way back in the nineteen-nineties, the Internet was just a bizarre novelty— noisy to access, clunky to navigate, as virginal as its users. *New Yorker* cartoons from that era convey confusion at its purported appeal. Take, for instance, a rock flying at the cranium of Tom Cheney's caveman: "You've got mail." Soon enough, however, the virtual world evolved to be predominant. Cartoons were forced to adapt. Their tone shifted in the twenty-first century: perplexity gave way to

"You've got mail."

TOM CHENEY, APRIL 19, 1999

grudging acceptance, which finally ceded to weary surrender. The World Wide Web won. But its ubiquity, instead of quashing cartoon humor, has furnished infinite fodder. Relationships, business, food, sports, sex—all the classic themes are refreshed. In a sense, **the Internet has turned us all into amateur cartoonists:** we've become isolated composers of Instagram captions, Twitter quips, and Facebook barbs. ♦

"I thought I'd be a successful fashion blogger by now."

"Remember when, on the Internet, nobody knew who you were?"

TOP BRUCE KAPLAN, AUGUST 4, 2014   BOTTOM KAAMRAN HAFEEZ, FEBRUARY 23, 2015

*SEE ALSO FACEBOOK, GOOGLE, TWITTER

"I feel like my best passwords are already behind me."

"But the Wi-Fi kept cutting out.
The only choice they had left was to unplug the router,
wait ten seconds, and THEN PLUG IT BACK IN!"

TOP DREW DERNAVICH, NOVEMBER 10, 2014   BOTTOM FARLEY KATZ, AUGUST 22, 2016

"It's good to get hammered by something other than the economy."

"When a wine rates over ninety, this is not alcoholism."

TOP FRANK COTHAM, OCTOBER 12, 2009 BOTTOM WILLIAM HAMILTON, MARCH 7, 2011

"You need to stop focusing on getting drunk and start focusing on being drunk."

THE HOME OF THE BOTTOMLESS MARTINI

TOP PAUL NOTH, JULY 23, 2007   BOTTOM MICK STEVENS, NOVEMBER 5, 2007

"I guess what I miss most is being drunk."

FRANK COTHAM, JANUARY 27, 1997

"*Never get a tattoo when you're drunk and hungry.*"

"*Biggers, two more Luau Sizzlers for Annie and me
and another Fog Cutter for Mrs. Grindstaff.*"

TOP ALEX GREGORY, SEPTEMBER 2, 2002 BOTTOM GEORGE BOOTH, NOVEMBER 27, 1978

"You're going to get a great summation! He's smashed!"

"Here's that bird you used to see when you were a drunk."

TOP ROWLAND WILSON, OCTOBER 27, 1962   BOTTOM ERIK HILGERDT, DECEMBER 11, 2006

*SEE ALSO BARS, LIGHT BULB IDEA, QUESTIONS

"I want to see other hallucinations."

"I doubt that a children's book about beer would sell."

TOP PAUL NOTH, MARCH 10, 2008   BOTTOM FRANK COTHAM, JANUARY 22, 2007

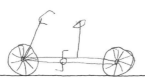

"It's the latest thing—warmth without weight."

*"If you ask me, the fire has the most potential,
but it's the smoke that has people talking."*

TOP ROBERT WEBER, JANUARY 29, 1990   BOTTOM JOHN CALDWELL, MARCH 29, 1999

GEORGE BOOTH, FEBRUARY 4, 1980

"My next big project is brakes."

SAM GROSS, MAY 12, 2008

WHO CAME UP WITH THAT?

OR *NEW YORKER* CARTOONISTS, the inventions of fire and the wheel supply a spark of inspiration that never fades. Jokes keep rolling off the pen. They're so inexhaustible that Matthew Diffee pokes fun at the sheer fatigue from their over-use. "Og discovered fire, and Thorak invented the wheel. There's nothing left for us," a caveman complains to his cavepal, but really he's speaking for the artist who craves different material. Still, **you can't escape your past,** and early inventors and contemporary inkers face the same challenge: a blank page, a formless rock, or a pile of twigs, each waiting to be transformed. Innovation, of course, has its perils, as we learn from an instant classic by Sam Gross, who depicts his cavemen running downhill, away from their newly chiseled tire. "My next big project is brakes," one says. Good luck. If history is any guide, there's no stopping these tropes anytime soon. ♦

*"Og discovered fire, and Thorak invented the wheel.
There's nothing left for us."*

"It looks O.K. But how are you going to hit people with it?"

TOP MATTHEW DIFFEE, MAY 14, 2007   BOTTOM JOSEPH MIRACHI, APRIL 3, 1971

"It's not supposed to do anything. It's just a study in abstract form."

WHEN THE INVENTOR OF THE WHEEL MET THE INVENTOR OF THE DEAL

TOP WHITNEY DARROW, JR., MAY 8, 1971 BOTTOM LEE LORENZ, AUGUST 22, 1988

"*Know what I dread? Inventory.*"

"*Gentlemen, we're sitting on a hell of a lot of inventory.*"

TOP ROBERT DAY, NOVEMBER 14, 1953   BOTTOM BERNARD SCHOENBAUM, DECEMBER 4, 1989

"And yet they still go right on writing them."

"I appreciate your contribution to our tremendous drawdown
of inventory, but isn't your office getting cramped?"

TOP ALAIN, MAY 12, 1956   BOTTOM P.C. VEY, APRIL 15, 2002

"Ready, Phil? Inventory time!"

BARNEY TOBEY, FEBRUARY 22, 1982

"All these people you invited—
are they friends or just inventory?"

"Funny what turns up when you take inventory."

"We might seize this opportunity, Mr. Grout,
to take an inventory."

TOP RICHARD CLINE, DECEMBER 6, 1999 MIDDLE NED HILTON, OCTOBER 12, 1935 BOTTOM GARRETT PRICE, SEPTEMBER 13, 1930

WARREN MILLER, SEPTEMBER 5, 1977

JACK & JILL
JACK-IN-THE-BOX
JARGON
JAZZ
JEALOUSY
JESTERS
JESUS
JEWELRY
JOB INTERVIEWS
JOGGING
JOUSTING
JUDGES

"I hereby pronounce you Jack and Jill. You may now go up the hill."

*"Let's just say you both went up this hill to fetch a pail of water,
then Jack fell down and broke his crown, and you, Jill, came tumbling after.
With this policy, you'd be covered for that."*

TOP J.B. HANDELSMAN, JANUARY 31, 1977   BOTTOM MICHAEL MASLIN, AUGUST 13, 2012

"Jack, when we get down the hill, let's put the pail up for auction."

"It's a long way to go for a pail of water."

TOP BRUCE KAPLAN, APRIL 2, 2001   BOTTOM ROBERT KRAUS, APRIL 3, 1965

TOP ROZ CHAST, JANUARY 23, 2017   BOTTOM EDWARD FRASCINO, AUGUST 7, 1995

*SEE ALSO HANSEL & GRETEL, MOUNTAIN CLIMBING

CHARLES ADDAMS, NOVEMBER 16, 1957

WALTER, FROM ACCOUNTING, IN-THE-BOX

MOLVIG

TOP ARIEL MOLVIG, DECEMBER 24, 2007   BOTTOM AL ROSS, APRIL 16, 1979

TOP SAUL STEINBERG, MARCH 5, 1960   BOTTOM OTTO SOGLOW, FEBRUARY 26, 1966

ROZ CHAST, MAY 7, 2007

"Take my advice, Haskins, and keep your out-of-the-box ideas to yourself."

TOP SAUL STEINBERG, NOVEMBER 19, 1960   BOTTOM CHARLES BARSOTTI, SEPTEMBER 7, 1998

"*It sounds a little too perfect. What's the downside?*"

"*There are exceptions. Sometimes it's possible to have buzz without any hype whatsoever.*"

TOP BERNARD SCHOENBAUM, SEPTEMBER 5, 1994   BOTTOM WILLIAM HAEFELI, JANUARY 19, 1998

"We beat the spread!"

"I got eight to twelve years, which was in line with Wall Street expectations."

TOP PAT BYRNES, JANUARY 16, 2006   BOTTOM LEO CULLUM, AUGUST 1, 2005

"Gentlemen, we are now playing hardball."

"Garbage in, garbage out!"

TOP GEORGE PRICE, JULY 7, 1986   BOTTOM GAHAN WILSON, AUGUST 23, 1993

"Miss Kessler is our poison pill here at Tolan, Merle & Fender."

"You know what I'd like to do, Caslow? I'd like to create a far-reaching, innovative program that will open a lot of channels, offer great opportunities, link up with all kinds of things, and enable something or other to happen. Any ideas?"

TOP LEE LORENZ, AUGUST 19, 1985 BOTTOM JAMES STEVENSON, APRIL 22, 1985

*"There are few moments in music so thrilling as when
Brucie and Mrs. Ritterhouse start riffing in tandem."*

*"If I had it all to do over again,
I would have liked to be the King of Swing."*

TOP GEORGE BOOTH, FEBRUARY 23, 1976   BOTTOM DANA FRADON, APRIL 17, 1978

"Come on, get hot!"

"Pop, tell me again how jazz came up the river from New Orleans."

TOP JAMES THURBER, APRIL 4, 1936   BOTTOM ELDON DEDINI, OCTOBER 19, 1957

"*Do you ever have days when you wish
you had a saxophone?*"

TOP CHON DAY, JULY 12, 1976   MIDDLE LEE LORENZ, NOVEMBER 15, 1969   BOTTOM SIDNEY HARRIS, JULY 9, 1973

*SEE ALSO CLASSICAL MUSIC, ROCK & ROLL, SONG LYRICS

BOB MANKOFF, OCTOBER 29, 1979

"*Sweetheart, I don't want anyone to make you unhappy except me.*"

"*He'll fasten his seat belt when I tell him to fasten his seat belt.*"

TOP BOB MANKOFF, JULY 6, 1998 BOTTOM JOSEPH MIRACHI, MARCH 3, 1973

"*This gentleman was kind enough to see me home, darling.*"

"*I noticed you were showing Marsha Hornbeck your whimsical side.*"

TOP JAMES THURBER, APRIL 4, 1936   BOTTOM CHARLES SAXON, AUGUST 7, 1978

"Don't be silly, darling! It's just somebody I knew in the Movement."

"I heard you telling that big blonde her perceptions were astonishingly vital."

TOP WILLIAM HAMILTON, APRIL 1, 1974   BOTTOM CHARLES SAXON, APRIL 9, 1960

"Have you ever coveted another man's wife, Sylvester?"

"Honey, this is Jack. He's the one who taught me how to do that thing you like."

TOP STAN HUNT, FEBRUARY 3, 1962   BOTTOM HARRY BLISS, APRIL 23, 2007

"*King me!*"

"*Your remote control, sire.*"

TOP JACK ZIEGLER, OCTOBER 28, 1985   BOTTOM MATTHEW DIFFEE, NOVEMBER 12, 2007

"I keep hoping he'll get tired of that reality stuff."

"Didn't this use to be the time slot for his news briefings?"

TOP PAUL NOTH, APRIL 14, 2008   BOTTOM DANA FRADON, APRIL 22, 2002

"Angelo tells us you haven't been laughing."

"My joke!"

TOP JOE DATOR, JUNE 4, 2012   BOTTOM MIKE TWOHY, AUGUST 31, 2009

"He gets all his news from us."

"See, things look a lot less funny sitting there, don't they?"

TOP MIKE TWOHY, OCTOBER 29, 2012   BOTTOM FRANK MODELL, DECEMBER 19, 1983

"Sorry, folks, but your insurance doesn't cover
more than one day in the manger."

"Thomas! Did Judas put you up to that?"

TOP J.B. HANDELSMAN, DECEMBER 15, 1997   BOTTOM JACK ZIEGLER, DECEMBER 1, 2014

"Being around Jesus brings out all my apostle issues."

TOP JACK ZIEGLER, MAY 1, 2006   BOTTOM BRUCE KAPLAN, APRIL 5, 2004

"*Now we'll need a sitter for New Year's Eve.*"

TOP LEO CULLUM, MARCH 29, 2004 MIDDLE SIDNEY HARRIS, DECEMBER 28, 1998 BOTTOM TOM CHENEY, SEPTEMBER 27, 1993

*SEE ALSO BIBLE, HEAVEN, RELIGION

"I've accepted him as my personal trainer."

"Did Jesus create these locally?"

TOP ERIC LEWIS, NOVEMBER 22, 2004   BOTTOM PAUL NOTH, NOVEMBER 8, 2010

*"There's an amusing little legend connected with it—
something about a dreadful curse."*

"I'm putting you on two earrings."

TOP CHARLES ADDAMS, JUNE 12, 1954   BOTTOM MISCHA RICHTER, JULY 3, 1989

"I know how expensive women's shoes are, but take the goddam jewelry!"

"Emeralds! Aren't they divine? Jack gave them to me to shut up about Women's Lib."

TOP ALEX GREGORY, SEPTEMBER 8, 2008   BOTTOM WILLIAM HAMILTON, AUGUST 22, 1970

"You know what you have?
You have awfully good taste, Marvin. I really mean it!"

"That's out of my price range. Do you have anything that's free?"

TOP FRANK MODELL, OCTOBER 10, 1970   BOTTOM MIKE TWOHY, NOVEMBER 28, 2005

*"You should wear a little jewelry with your overalls,
sweetheart, so people don't get the wrong idea."*

"My jewelry's all wearing out."

TOP ROBERT WEBER, JANUARY 3, 1977   BOTTOM BARBARA SHERMUND, MARCH 5, 1938

"I gotta tell ya, these embezzlement convictions raise a red flag."

"And you can assure me that you're right in the head <u>now</u>?"

TOP BOB MANKOFF, APRIL 3, 1995   BOTTOM FRANK COTHAM, MARCH 25, 1996

"I can see from your résumé that you're a man."

"Of course, with the position that has the benefits—
medical, dental, et cetera—there is no salary."

TOP HARRY BLISS, MARCH 17, 2014   BOTTOM WARREN MILLER, AUGUST 17, 1992

J

WHAT CAN I TELL YOU?

WHERE DO YOU SEE YOURSELF in the next five years? A job interview puts you on the spot. *What's your biggest weakness?* The notion that you can condense everything there is to know about yourself into a one-page résumé and a thirty-minute interview is patently ridiculous. *What can you tell us about yourself?* Cartoons about this necessity of professional life have to **condense that ridiculousness into a single picture and maybe a dozen-word caption.** *How would you describe your current position?* These cartoons tend to be accurate barometers of the economic climate in which they were created, reflecting particularly the optimism or pessimism of the job market. *If you could be any kind of animal, which one would it be?* And they make a permanent record of an era's peculiar tropes and work ethos. *What makes you think you'll fit in here?* So, if you're looking for good company for your or a co-worker's feelings of inadequacy, rejection, or under-appreciation, a cartoon might do the job nicely. *What are your laughter requirements?* ♦

"You don't look like a Dave."

MIKE TWOHY, FEBRUARY 29, 1988

"Sorry. We don't need anyone at the moment."

"So, Jim, where do you see yourself in ten minutes?"

TOP DREW DERNAVICH, MARCH 16, 2009   BOTTOM MATTHEW DIFFEE, JULY 9, 2001

"Right now it's between you and two hundred and fifty other people who came to Seattle, moved in with five roommates, joined a band, took a job in a coffee bar, got fed up, had a meeting with themselves, and decided it was time to go out and get a real job."

"The years 1966 through 1995 are blank because I was on tour with the Grateful Dead."

TOP DAVID SIPRESS, MARCH 28, 2011   BOTTOM JACK ZIEGLER, OCTOBER 9, 1995

"Hi, you wouldn't happen to have some change on you?
I'm trying to get a shot of carrot juice."

"No horse this morning, Brewster. I'm jogging around myself."

TOP FRANK MODELL, APRIL 26, 1976   BOTTOM WARREN MILLER, JUNE 1, 1968

"Pass 'em, Pop."

TOP HARRY BLISS, MAY 17, 2010   BOTTOM BOB MANKOFF, APRIL 3, 1989

"To think that all these years I've been jogging without even knowing it!"

TOP CHARLES BARSOTTI, JULY 31, 1978 BOTTOM JAMES STEVENSON, MAY 18, 1968

"*Anything wrong?*"

JEAN SEMPÉ, NOVEMBER 2, 1981

TOP SAUL STEINBERG, JANUARY 18, 1964   BOTTOM JACK ZIEGLER, OCTOBER 13, 2003

TOP CHRISTOPHER WEYANT, JULY 14, 2003   BOTTOM LIAM WALSH, DECEMBER 8, 2014

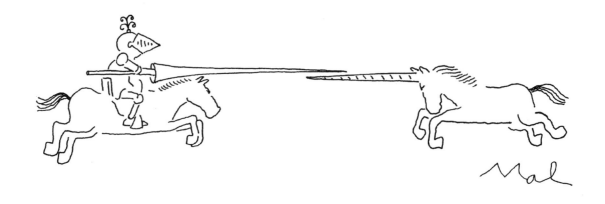

TOP MISCHA RICHTER, MARCH 8, 1976   MIDDLE LEE LORENZ, JANUARY 16, 1989   BOTTOM MALCOLM HANCOCK, JULY 4, 1977

TOP WARREN MILLER, APRIL 15, 1991   BOTTOM LESLIE STARKE, SEPTEMBER 8, 1951

"*And don't go whining to some higher court.*"

"*Do you ever have one of those days when everything seems unconstitutional?*"

TOP AL ROSS, NOVEMBER 9, 1998   BOTTOM JOSEPH MIRACHI, DECEMBER 30, 1974

*"Since you have already been convicted by the media,
I imagine we can wrap this up pretty quickly."*

"Recess is over, Your Honor."

TOP MISCHA RICHTER, AUGUST 5, 1991   BOTTOM MICK STEVENS, FEBRUARY 24, 1997

OVERRULED

J UDGE NOT LEST ye be judged, or jeered. Is there anyone more ripe for ridicule than that black-robed, gavel-wielding demigod who presides over the fate of the powerless? The judge and the cartoonist are ideal counterparts. **The jurist and the satirist—together they keep a delicate balance.** It's irresistible to poke fun at the pomp, the solemnity, and the circumlocutions of courtroom etiquette and its arbiter, all the more so because the decrees are deadly serious. Even a schoolyard pun will do. "Recess is over, Your Honor," Mick Stevens's dutiful bailiff informs a judge who's playing on a swing set. A gag cartoonist would probably make an inappropriate courtroom sketch artist, going for the laugh and not the likeness, although he or she might draw nearer to the truth. "Do you ever have one of those days when everything seems unconstitutional?" Joseph Mirachi's mustachioed justice muses. Guilty as charged. As long as our society is governed by laws, we'll need cartoonists to thumb their noses at those whose thumbs are on the scales of justice. ♦

"The Court will allow the cape but will draw the line at the wind machine."

DREW DERNAVICH, MAY 10, 2010

"As it's coming on winter, I suggest we recess until spring."

"The jury will disregard the witness's last remarks."

TOP MICHAEL MASLIN, OCTOBER 26, 1992 BOTTOM LEE LORENZ, OCTOBER 3, 1977

*"In the interest of streamlining the judicial process,
we'll skip the evidence and go directly to sentencing."*

J.B. HANDELSMAN, JANUARY 16, 1995

FRANK MODELL, SEPTEMBER 10, 1966

KANGAROOS
KANSAS
KARATE
KAYAKS
KETCHUP
KING ARTHUR
KING KONG
KISSING
KITES
KITTENS
KLEPTOMANIA
KLUTZES
KNIGHTS
KNITTING

"And you call yourself a marsupial?"

"He's got to be in here <u>somewhere!</u>"

TOP LEO CULLUM, JULY 11, 1988   BOTTOM KENNETH MAHOOD, JUNE 10, 1991

"Perhaps __this__ will refresh your memory."

"Remember now, __you__ got the brains."

TOP JAMES THURBER, APRIL 6, 1935   BOTTOM GEORGE PRICE, FEBRUARY 15, 1941

"Perhaps you have some other kind of court to suggest?"

"In your ad you said you'd grown up in the shade of a coolibah tree. How so?"

TOP ED FISHER, SEPTEMBER 5, 1970   BOTTOM VICTORIA ROBERTS, DECEMBER 15, 1997

TOP LIANA FINCK, JULY 31, 2017   BOTTOM EDWARD KOREN, APRIL 29, 1991

"Let me know at once when we're over Kansas. I was born in Kansas."

"He's got to be in here somewhere!"

TOP GARRETT PRICE, APRIL 7, 1956   BOTTOM MICK STEVENS, FEBRUARY 13, 2012

TOP JACK ZIEGLER, SEPTEMBER 5, 2016 BOTTOM BOB MANKOFF, FEBRUARY 26, 1979

"Why does she want to go back to Kansas, where everything is in black-and-white?"

EDWARD FRASCINO, JANUARY 2, 1989

"Ooh, you have a tornado right <u>there</u>."

*"Tell us again how you took five thousand head out to Kansas City
and made it back in time to pick up the kids from gymnastics."*

TOP CHARLES BARSOTTI, MAY 27, 1996   BOTTOM JOHN KLOSSNER, FEBRUARY 27, 2012

K

"Harcourt, here, has a black belt in budget management."

TOP GEORGE PRICE, FEBRUARY 22, 1964   BOTTOM LEE LORENZ, MAY 25, 1981

LEARN KARATE

"How long will it be before I feel that I own the night?"

GEORGE BOOTH, NOVEMBER 29, 1993

JAMES STEVENSON, JUNE 9, 1975

"Please, no karate chops this P.M., my little brown-belted pumpkin seed."

TOP LEO CULLUM, APRIL 3, 1989   BOTTOM WARREN MILLER, NOVEMBER 7, 1970

Two-Bedroom Kayak

TOP OTTO SOGLOW, MAY 25, 1957   BOTTOM ARNIE LEVIN, MARCH 24, 1980

"I can't go ashore. I haven't any pants on."

"It's Oglub's boat all right, but it doesn't look like Oglub."

TOP DOUGLAS BORGSTEDT, SEPTEMBER 21, 1935   BOTTOM OTTO SOGLOW, MARCH 7, 1953

"This seems just a trifle snug. May I try a size forty-six?"

RICHARD DECKER, NOVEMBER 14, 1931

"I can still fit into my high-school kayak."

TOP MISCHA RICHTER, DECEMBER 15, 1956 BOTTOM MATTHEW DIFFEE, SEPTEMBER 1, 2014

K

"Is there any ketchup in the house?"

TOP JACK ZIEGLER, JUNE 4, 1984   BOTTOM ARNIE LEVIN, JULY 31, 1978

"Ketchup please."

TOP WARREN MILLER, MAY 20, 1985   BOTTOM PETER ARNO, DECEMBER 5, 1925

"King Arthur is late, as usual."

TOP WARREN MILLER, SEPTEMBER 12, 1964   BOTTOM DANNY SHANAHAN, MAY 4, 2009

"Let's make the bill easy and just split it."

"I'm going to need to speak to someone from either personnel or maintenance."

TOP ARNIE LEVIN, FEBRUARY 22, 1988   BOTTOM CHRISTOPHER WEYANT, APRIL 17, 2006

K

Despite some initial reservations, the knights were often grateful
for Guinevere's presence at the Round Table.

TOP CHARLES ADDAMS, DECEMBER 5, 1964   BOTTOM J.B. HANDELSMAN, FEBRUARY 1, 1993

"Sorry. Next!"

*"I am the Lady of the Lake, and because thou hast defiled my crystal waters
I must hence smite thee. That or penalize thee a stroke. Your call."*

TOP SAM GROSS, JULY 14, 1975   BOTTOM PAT BYRNES, MAY 31, 1999

"He thinks he's so great!"

TOP WHITNEY DARROW, JR., FEBRUARY 4, 1961   BOTTOM DANNY SHANAHAN, JULY 17, 1989

"*Did you hear what happened to King Kong?*"

TOP JOSEPH FARRIS, JANUARY 10, 1977   BOTTOM JASON PATTERSON, MARCH 16, 2009

LIVING LARGE

IF YOU THINK there have been a lot of movies starring King Kong since the original film was released in 1933, you may want to sit down before you hear how often he's stumbled into cartoons. **The misunderstood beast that just wanted to hang out at home** (who can't sympathize?) has scaled a peak perhaps even higher than the Empire State Building by being a cartoon trope. He's confused; so are we. Having taken him from his natural habitat, we react to him in the way we always react to the strangers we fear. But this furry creature doesn't want to destroy; he just wants to escape. No matter: cartoons don't give up their captives.

Like poor King Kong, the trope broke from its chains to go to new places; in a 1998 cartoon by J.B. Handelsman, Le Roi Kong is shown scaling Le Tour Eiffel. In the end, Kong is just like us, whether he's hanging out with his monster buddies or— as posited by Joe Dator in 2010—feeling overwhelmed because the city is too full of twee bakeries. Once again, cartooning apes life. ♦

"It wasn't the airplanes. 'Twas all these goddam cupcake places killed the beast."

JOE DATOR, OCTOBER 25, 2010

TOP TOM HACHTMAN, MARCH 13, 2000 BOTTOM CHARLES ADDAMS, DECEMBER 20, 1976

*SEE ALSO GODZILLA, NEW YORK CITY, THE THREE MONKEYS

Le Roi Kong

J.B. HANDELSMAN, APRIL 27, 1998

"Sometimes, Martha, you defy analysis."

TOP ELDON DEDINI, JULY 4, 1977 BOTTOM ROBERT WEBER, NOVEMBER 14, 1977

"May I help you?"

"We had that in school last week."

TOP FRANK MODELL, OCTOBER 17, 1964   BOTTOM BARNEY TOBEY, NOVEMBER 8, 1969

TOP CHON DAY, JUNE 15, 1963   BOTTOM WILLIAM STEIG, MARCH 30, 1968

*SEE ALSO DATING, SEX, TUNNEL OF LOVE

"You don't know how thankful I am that he doesn't spend it on candy."

TOP WARREN MILLER, JUNE 17, 1972   BOTTOM CLAUDE SMITH, AUGUST 13, 1960

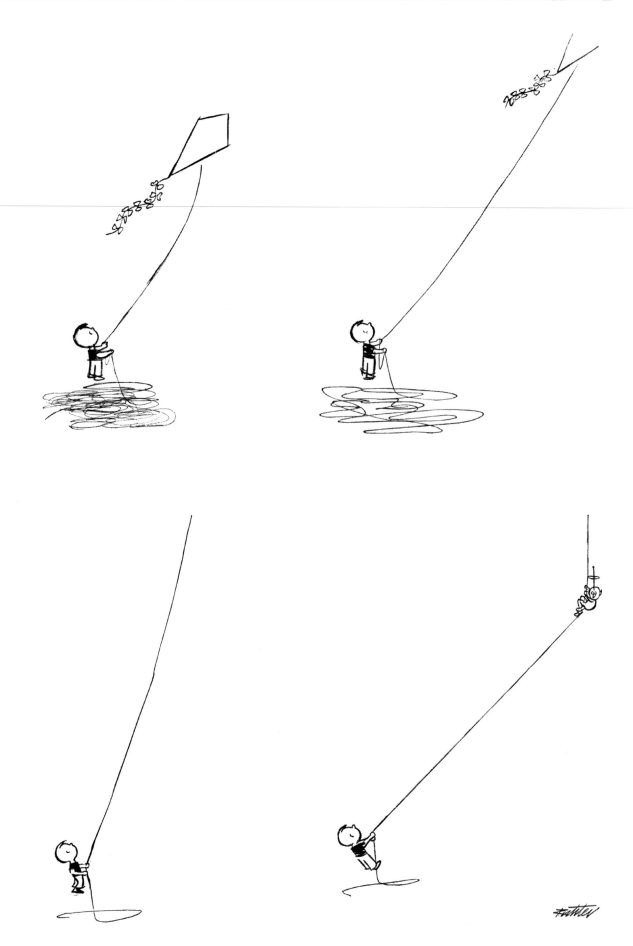

MISCHA RICHTER, JUNE 1, 1963

"Hey, Ben! We're in Maine now. We don't have to perform."

LEISURE TIME

TOP MICHAEL CRAWFORD, JULY 26, 1993   BOTTOM CHARLES BARSOTTI, APRIL 19, 1982

"This is humiliating. Couldn't you drop me a block from school?"

"If you must know, Jimmy, you came from a box
in front of the market. It said 'Free Kittens.'"

TOP LEO CULLUM, MAY 15, 2000   BOTTOM LEO CULLUM, JULY 19, 1993

S. GROSS

"Can I borrow those kittens for an hour?
I want to freak out the people who had me spayed."

"Mrs. Wallace _made_ me take them. She said they were as much ours as theirs."

TOP SAM GROSS, MAY 24, 1999   BOTTOM GARRETT PRICE, MARCH 28, 1953

K

SAUL STEINBERG, DECEMBER 30, 1950

*SEE ALSO CAT VS. MOUSE, DOGS VS. CATS, GOLDFISH BOWLS

"It's kittens."

TOP SAM GROSS, AUGUST 21, 1989   BOTTOM PETER STEINER, MARCH 11, 1991

"Mr. Hallock!"

TOP JOHN O'BRIEN, NOVEMBER 6, 2000   BOTTOM DANA FRADON, SEPTEMBER 3, 1960

"This isn't about your stealing anything. It's about your not buying anything."

"That's rather a poor start at a shoplifting career, Madam."

TOP DREW DERNAVICH, NOVEMBER 17, 2014   BOTTOM GEORGE PRICE, JULY 2, 1938

"What, no veggies?"

"That'll be sixty-eight ninety. Madame has on two hats."

TOP BILL WOODMAN, MARCH 16, 1998   BOTTOM CLAUDE SMITH, DECEMBER 5, 1953

"Gosh, Chuck, I don't know. I suppose what I miss more
than anything else is stealing."

ROBERT WEBER, NOVEMBER 2, 1963

"See what I mean? He's his own worst enemy."

"Well, none of the rest of us ever bump our heads!"

TOP ROBERT DAY, JUNE 25, 1955   BOTTOM GAHAN WILSON, FEBRUARY 7, 1977

"Are you going to fall off that damn stool every time he hits a clinker?"

"There they go, the Four Horsemen—
Famine, Pestilence, Death, and Butterfingers."

TOP GEORGE PRICE, JANAURY 20, 1951   BOTTOM PETER ARNO, NOVEMBER 25, 1967

K

"It's all right. I just tripped on the last step."

ROBERT DAY, JULY 7, 1951

*SEE ALSO DANCE, JESTERS

"I don't know. Poor Arthur has lived, but he's never learned."

"A lot of good it does saying 'Have a good day' to you!"

TOP KENNETH MAHOOD, OCTOBER 9, 1971   BOTTOM FRANK MODELL, JUNE 3, 1972

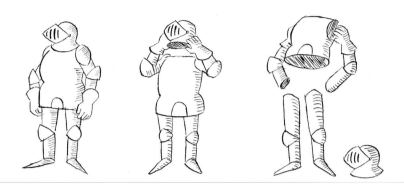

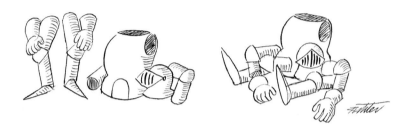

*"Stop grumbling! If you're going to have knights in shining armor,
someone's got to shine the armor."*

TOP MISCHA RICHTER, NOVEMBER 28, 1964 BOTTOM JAMES STEVENSON, NOVEMBER 2, 1963

"*Don't you see, Roland, being a knight in shining armor isn't enough.
All the fellows I know are knights in shining armor.*"

WARREN MILLER, JUNE 6, 1964

CHRISTOPHER WEYANT, AUGUST 9, 1999

"I love the patter of raindrops on my helmet."

"When I ask questions, I expect answers!"

TOP LEONARD DOVE, OCTOBER 1, 1960   BOTTOM EDWARD KOREN, SEPTEMBER 21, 1987

TOP CHARLES ADDAMS, MARCH 11, 1974   BOTTOM HENRY MARTIN, MARCH 5, 1979

"Tell me, Agnes, just what the hell __have__ you been knitting all these years?"

TOP BARNEY TOBEY, OCTOBER 13, 1975 BOTTOM WARREN MILLER, JULY 29, 1972

A STITCH IN TIME

KNITTING APPEARS TO be on the cusp—or should we say cuff?—of a cultural come-back. Urban hipsters do it between subway stops. Yarn-bombing is a popular way to beautify public spaces. Crochet is no longer a hobby exclusive to the crotchety. So why haven't *New Yorker* cartoons kept up with the times? For many decades, the maga-zine was thickly woven with traditional wisecracks on the subject. **Housewives wielded needles while needling their husbands;** a Puritan home-maker, for example, makes the most of her spouse's confinement in the stockade by using his hands for a spool. She even seems to prefer it—which is the detail of Warren Miller's drawing that puts you in stitches. But, after the nineteen-seventies, knitting jokes went out of fashion, much like the chore of mending socks. Darn it! A new generation of cartoonists may revive the genre in its trendy, retro, ungendered form. Until then, we wait with knitted brows. ♦

ALAIN, JANUARY 7, 1950

"Thank you kindly, sonny, but I already have an agent."

"You keep him busy while I go for help."

TOP DONALD REILLY, OCTOBER 29, 1973   BOTTOM SAM GROSS, APRIL 16, 2007

CROSS-COUNTRY KNITTING

ROZ CHAST, JUNE 12, 1989